Hornsea
A Century Ago

The Town and its People in the 1890s

Editor: M. H. Smith

Hornsea Local History Class

Highgate Publications (Beverley) Ltd
1993

British Library Cataloguing in Publication Data available

© 1993

ISBN 0 948929 82 0

Published by
Highgate Publications (Beverley) Ltd.
24 Wylies Road, Beverley, HU17 7AP
Telephone (0482) 866826

Produced by
B. A. Print
4 Newbegin, Lairgate, Beverley, HU17 8EG
Telephone (0482) 886017

Preface

This book consists of a series of studies made by members of the Hornsea W.E.A. Local History Class on different aspects of the town's progress in the closing decade of the 19th century. Each study represented a separate project and, occasionally, items of information in one chapter were repeated in another. However, not all the duplicated information has been edited out because the group felt that, firstly, each chapter could then be read in isolation without reference to other parts of the book and, secondly, the reader would be in a position to realise how different aspects of Hornsea's history were often influenced by the same people or the same events.

Although the separate topics were discussed by all the members of the group, each chapter has been the main responsibility of just a part of the group. The compilers of the various chapters were: Chapter 2, Geoff Strangward; Chapter 3, Joan Wise, Peggy Wood and Bernard Wise; Chapter 4, Harry Sharp; Chapter 5, William Browning; Chapter 6, George White; Chapter 7, Anne Malley and Les Jackson; Chapter 8, Pat Browning; Chapter 9, Alf Maltby; Chapter 10, Maureen Mallison; Chapters 1 and 11, the editor. With the photographs of old Hornsea we have been much helped by Mr. E. J. (Jim) Hobson, not only in supplying the photographs but also in identifying some of the people and objects featured on them. He has also had some helpful comments to make on the text. We would also like to acknowledge the help of the staff at the Humberside County Record Office in Beverley and the permission of the Controller of H. M. Stationery Office to use reproductions of the Hornsea census returns, which are Crown copyright and which were provided by Humberside Leisure Services (Public Record Office document reference RG12/3951). Our thanks go particularly to our sponsors and patrons, British Gas, Hornsea Town Council, Holderness Borough Council, Rise Farms and the East Yorkshire Local History Society, who have supported the publication of this book financially.

Finally, may I say on behalf of the Hornsea Local History Class that we have very much enjoyed compiling this book and hope that the reader will just as much enjoy reading it.

Maitland Smith
September, 1993

Visit Michael at:

Ye Olde Cottage Cafe

for your
morning coffee
lunch and
afternoon teas

Newbegin, Hornsea

**To the memory of
Geoff Strangward,
who died
September 20th, 1993**

Woodstock Designs Ltd
The Kitchen, Bedroom and Bathroom Specialists

Free design and quotations

Head Office - Factory - Showroom
**Aldborough Road
Withernwick
HU11 4TF
Tel: (0964) 527889**

Hornsea Showroom
**10 Southgate Court
Hornsea
HU18 1RP
Tel: (0964) 536609**

J. R. Gelsthorpe

Specialist in long case and wall clocks

Prompt full and part house clearances arranged

Immediate cash settlement

Residence:
35 Market Place, Hornsea
Workshop and carpark at rear
Entrance on Mereside

Tel: (0964) 535201

David Bond

Hornsea's longest established Gentlemen's Hairdresser

Hornsea Born - Established 1956

Kevin Bond

Qualified Ladies Hair Stylist

Southgate, Hornsea
Tel: 533991

C. J. Evans
THE JEWELLERS

72 Southgate
Hornsea
East Yorkshire
Telephone: (0964) 533172

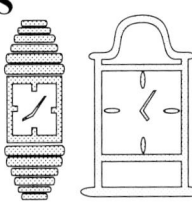

ALL YOUR GIFT REQUIREMENTS IN GOLD AND SILVER
WITH A FINE SELECTION OF
CLOCKS, WATCHES AND SILVER PLATE
Valuations for insurance and probate
Fast and efficient repair service

PRESCRIPTIONS

We offer a complete prescription service including - hosiery, oxygen and homeopathy
FREE DELIVERIES of repeat prescriptions willingly made. Simply ask us

Stephen P. Bowling

VANTAGE
CHEMIST

OPEN: 8.45 am - 6.00 pm Monday - Friday; 8.45 am - 5.00 pm Saturday

85 NEWBEGIN, HORNSEA. Tel: 532066

The best from the sea direct to your table

Sullivans

Finest Quality Fish and Chips

OPEN
SEVEN DAYS
A WEEK

TO TAKE AWAY OR EAT IN OUR
LICENSED RESTAURANT

34-38 New Road, Hornsea. Tel: 0964 534118

1 — Census Day, 1891

The census of Great Britain in 1891 was carried out on the eve and morning of Monday, 6 April. The previous Monday had been Easter Bank Holiday and no doubt the Government considered that, on the 6th, the great majority of the population would be in their places of residence and the returns would give as accurate a picture of the population as it was possible to obtain.

At Hornsea during the previous week the children of the National School, down by the Mere, had returned to school on the Tuesday after having Good Friday and Easter Monday as a holiday. As they had broken up on the Thursday afternoon the master of the school had been proud to report that several children had actually asked for Arithmetic cards so that they could prepare for the visit of Her Majesty's Inspector who was due in a fortnight's time.

It had been a cold year so far, one in a series over the last 15 years. In the January a cricket match had been played on the ice of Hornsea Mere, something which had become almost a tradition of late (ox-roasts had been held on the ice in 1875 and 1884). An entry in the school log for January 1891 recorded that one of the lads playing truant had fallen in a swan-hole in the ice and perished. Later in the month the master ascribed the low attendance to the fact that some of the children were afraid to come on account of the cold. On Easter Sunday, the week before the census, there was snow in Holderness. The cold weather was to continue through the year. In the May and the June it was to be so cold on occasions that it

Market Place, Hornsea, looking north. The gas lamp pillar on the left marked the dividing line between the areas covered by enumerators John Barr and Horace Miskin in the taking of the 1891 census. Horace Miskin took the area to the north of the lamp and, in fact, the first household on his census return was Richard Fisher's tailor's shop, seen on this photograph. The next shop was occupied by Hannah Leak, grocer. William Parker, grocer and provision merchant, had the next shop, and his horse-drawn van, which delivered goods to the surrounding villages, is seen outside the shop. At the far end of Market Place is Thomas Smith's butcher's shop with the Primitive Methodist chapel next to it. Robert Barr, plumber, glazier and painter, had the shop in the right foreground. Beyond his shop was Heslop's the chemist (still a chemist's shop). Note the condition of the roads. The photograph was taken after 1901, which was the year that most of Hornsea's pavements were flagged, although John Heslop had put stone flags in front of his shop as early as 1877. Previous to that the paths had been cobbled.

Part of the enumerator's return for Grosvenor Terrace, New Road. It indicates the considerable amount of information which the head of the household had to enter on the schedule. Numbers 7 and 8 Grosvenor Terrace (now Nos. 15 and 17 New Road) were where Miss Mary Skinner held her High School for Girls. Note the widespread origins of, not only Miss Skinner and her staff and pupils, but also some of the other residents and their servants.

was necessary to light the school fires. The cold eventually brought some cause for rejoicing to the children, however, when they received an extra week's holiday in the September in order to help with the delayed harvest.

With snow on Easter Sunday, it was unlikely that Hornsea was flooded with visitors on Bank Holiday Monday. However, an attraction seemed to be in the offing. Early in the week the town was placarded with posters announcing that a grand parachute descent by Professor Norris was to take place on the promenade at 12.30 on Wednesday. By noon that day a goodly number of people had gathered expectantly on the promenade — a wide gravel drive which had only been laid out along the cliff top in the early part of that year. It was not until prospective viewers of the descent had waited around for an hour, with no sight of a balloon or the professor, that they realised it was April Fool's Day.

Events like these, and the weather, no doubt gave the people of Hornsea something to talk about in the week leading up to the census. They also no doubt discussed the forms that were being distributed to each household during the week. These were the census forms, or schedules, which were being handed out and explained by the two enumerators covering the 414 inhabited houses in the parish of Hornsea-with-Burton. The enumerators were local men, both with experience of clerical duties. John Barr was the Registrar of Births, Marriages and Deaths, the Assessor and Collector of Income Tax and the Collector of the Poor Rate. In the taking of the census he was responsible for 'All that part of the Parish of Hornsea which Lies South of the Gas Lamp Pillar in the Market Place....' Horace Miskin was the parish clerk and had an ironmongery business in Newbegin. In the census he dealt with the part of Hornsea lying to the north of the gas lamp pillar.

In the week following the census, Barr and Miskin collected the schedules, helping the head of each household with any problems he or she may have had in completing the form. Problems there may well have been. The form asked for a lot of information: the name of each person residing in the house on the day of the census, their age, sex, marital status, their relation to the head of the family or their position in the household (e.g. servant, visitor or boarder), their occupation, place of birth, whether he or she was an employer of labour, an employee or neither, and whether he or she was deaf, dumb, blind or mentally handicapped. If the house had fewer than five occupied rooms then the number had to be stated. Comprehending all the questions and filling in the replies could have presented some form-fillers with difficulties. Elementary education had not been compulsory in England until after 1870 (it was not until 1884 that Hornsea formed a school board in order to enforce attendance at the National School) and up to 1891 had to be paid for by the parents. Some heads of households would have been illiterate and may have had to turn to their children for help in interpreting the questions and filling in the answers.

In the cases of old folk living alone the enumerators no doubt had to do most of the form-filling themselves.

After sorting out the problems the enumerators transferred the information from the schedules to their returns. They then totalled up the numbers of males and females, dwellings and households, and took the returns, along with all the schedules, to the local Registrar of Births, Marriages and Deaths. As already mentioned, this was John Barr, who had acted as one of the enumerators in Hornsea. Barr was a 47-year-old bachelor, living with his brother and his wife at Corner House in Eastgate. He was the first of a remarkable succession of members of the Barr family to act as Registrar in Hornsea, for he was succeeded by his nephew Harold who, in turn, was succeeded by his niece Marion, the three serving a total of over 80 years in the post.

As Registrar, John Barr's responsibilities during the census covered Hornsea and a number of villages

Corner House, Eastgate, where John Barr, the Registrar of Births, Marriages and Deaths, resided in 1891. Inset: John Barr. (The photograph of John Barr was kindly supplied by Mrs. Margaret Thorpe.)

around. All the enumerators from the area were instructed by him and he helped them to deal with any difficulties they may have encountered (such as what to do if anyone refused to fill in the schedule). The forms were then forwarded to the Superintendent Registrar at Beverley from where they were sent to the Registrar General in London. There, clerks and mathematicians calculated such things as the age ranges of the population in the different parts of the country, the percentages engaged in the various trades and occupations and many other statistics for use by government bodies. The householders' schedules were then destroyed and the enumerators' returns were sent to the Public Record Office for safe keeping, not to be viewed by the public for 100 whole years and a day after the taking of the census. Consequently, it was not until 2 January 1992 that the returns became available for general viewing. A few months later copies of the local returns were obtained by the Humberside County Record Office at Beverley. It was from these copies that the Hornsea W.E.A. Class obtained the information for the basis of this study.

The totals derived by Messrs. Barr and Miskin and entered on their returns showed Hornsea's population to be 2,013, a rise of nearly 10% from its figure of 1,836 in 1881. As in previous decades and as in most of the country, the female population outnumbered the males — in Hornsea by 1,142 to 871. Also in Hornsea, 115 of the 425 families lived in houses or apartments with fewer than five rooms.

The rise of nearly 10% in Hornsea's population since 1881 was almost the same increase as for the country as a whole: Great Britain's population had risen by exactly 10%, from 30 million to 33 million in the ten years. The change, however, was not uniform throughout the country. In the villages, including most of Hornsea's neighbours, whose economies were based mainly on agriculture, the population generally declined or stagnated. In the towns and cities, thriving on trade and manufacture, the population increased at greater than the national rate as people were drawn from the country by the greater availability of work. As we shall see in the following pages, some of Hornsea's population were engaged in manufacture, but that was only a small part of the reason for the modest prosperity reflected in the town's rising population. A stronger reason for the rise was Hornsea's link by rail to the swelling town of Hull and thence to the other prospering cities of the West Riding and further afield. For Hull, Hornsea provided a place of residence for some of its more well-to-do citizens. For the towns beyond Hull, as well as for Hull itself, Hornsea was another choice of seaside resort amongst the many which had grown up along the Yorkshire coast. Catering for visitors, although only a seasonal occupation, augmented the income of many families who might otherwise have followed the migration to the cities.

The population of Hornsea, 1801 to 1891

Year	1801	1811	1821	1831	1841	1851	1861	1871	1881	1891
Date	10/3	27/5	28/5	30/5	7/6	31/3	8/4	3/4	4/4	6/4
Population	533	704	790	780	1005	945	1063	1685	1836	2013

The population of Hornsea had climbed slowly but erratically since Britain's first census in 1801 (see Table). In that time the population of the country as a whole had increased steadily from 10.5 million to 33 million. Hornsea's population fluctuated for various reasons, but often because the census was taken at different times of the year. In 1821, when the census was at the end of May, the enumerator commented, 'Hornsea is resorted to as a bathing place; hence the increase in Inhabitants'. In 1851, when the census was at the end of March, the comment was, 'The season for visitors had not commenced when the census was taken'. There was a different reason for a low figure in 1831: 'Upwards of 100 persons have lately emigrated to America from Hornsea, notwithstanding which the Population is the same'. However, there was a genuine surge in the population in the decade between 1861 and 1871, when there was an increase of almost 60% following the opening of the Hull and Hornsea Railway in 1864. In the following two decades the rise continued but only at a rate approximating to the national rise, namely that due to the increase of births over deaths. However, this does not mean that there was no movement into Hornsea, but it does mean that those coming in were counterbalanced by those moving out. It was a gradually shifting scene, of which we have a glimpse on one day in April 1891.

The returns tell us a lot about each individual in Hornsea on that day 100 years ago — in which house he or she was residing, together with all the other information which the head of the household had entered on his schedule. The returns also give a glimpse of the housing conditions of the time — how many people were staying in each house on the night of 5 April and also, if the house had fewer than five rooms, how many rooms there were. In all, the returns reveal much interesting information about Hornsea and its people. In order to expand on that information, we have turned to other records: maps, plans, sketches and photographs to show the physical nature of the town; and such things as local newspapers and directories, school log books, the records of Church and Chapel, and the minutes of various local government bodies to tell us something of the town's inhabitants — their work, their religion, their social activities and their everyday life. The outcome, the story of Hornsea and its people a century ago, is told in the following pages.

The directories of the time helped to supplement the information from the census returns in preparing many of the chapters of this book. Part of the Hornsea section of Bulmer's Directory *for 1892.*

HORNSEA-WITH-BURTON PARISH.

TRADES AND PROFESSIONS.

Academies & Schools.
Bellerby Mrs. Sarah Ann (dame), Southgate
Hall Miss Emily K. (day), Public rooms
Holly Lodge (boys' classical & commercial—day & boarding); Henry Elsom (Lond. Univ.), principal; F. Bradford, assistant master
Leyland's (boys' day & boarding); John B. Ridges, M.A., principal; A. H. Scholefield, B.A., assistant master
National (mixed); Isaac Gilman, master; Misses L. B. Crowe and E. E. Stephenson, assistants; Infant — Miss Sarah Beall, mistress
Russell Mrs. Ombler (dame), Market place
Skinner Miss Mary (girls' day and boarding), Grosvenor house
Stone Miss Letitia R. (day—music, &c.), Sunbeam house

Bakers & Confectioners
Hall Allan (and refreshment rooms), Guild hs., Newbegin
Hobson Mrs. Edith, Southgate
Lott John, Newbegin
Norman John (and gravel merchant), Southgate

Banks.
Hornsea Penny Savings (open Saturdays, 7 to 8 p.m., winter, 3 to 4 p.m.), Public rooms
Post Office Savings
York City & County Banking Co. Ltd. (sub-branch) (open Monday's, 12 to 3 p.m.) (draw on Lloyd's, Ltd.), Market place

Blacksmiths.
Salmond Wilfred, Market place
Smith David, Market place
Stephenson Robert, Southgate

Boatbuilders.
Akester Jos. Ainley, Newbegin
Holmes Jas. T., Hornsea mere —(See Advt.)

Boot & Shoe Makers.
Arksey Thos. John, Bk. Southgate
Barton William, Southgate
Burnett Saml., the family boot warehouse, Newbegin—(See Advt.)
Garton Thomas, Southgate
Garton William, Newbegin
Howlett James, Market place
Lonsdale John, Market place
Robinson Wm. (& newsagent), Southgate
Scott Chas. (& letter carrier), Newbegin

Builders (Bricklayers).
Bennett George, Newbegin
Denton John (stone mason), Westgate
Grantham Henry, Southgate
Hulse (Henry) & Stephenson (Wm. Bennett), 1 Rise ter

Builders (Joiners.)
Allman George, 3 Marine ter
Barr Henry & Wm. Kemplay, Eastgate
Beall Robert Bell, Westgate
Foley Thomas, Mere side
Pickering Robert, Southgate

Butchers.
Bulson John (and farmer), Southgate
Burn Joseph Hume (and gravel merchant), Newbegin
Clark Thos. Wharf (and cattle dealer), Market place
Smith Thomas, Market place
Stephenson George, junior, Southgate

Cab Proprietors.
Barker Robert, Westgate
Dukes William, Newbegin
Hall (Thomas) & Son (Robert), Southgate
Langley Frederick, Southgate

Carriers.
Banks Edward, Mere walk
Carr Miss Rose, Eastgate
N.E. Railway Co. (general), W. Train, agent

Chemists.
(Marked * is also dentist.)
Heslop John, Market place
Loten Bros. (Arthur Richard and *Thos.) (and grocers), Grosvenor view & Market pl

Chimney Sweepers.
Johnson Chas., 9 Ocean ter
Outram James Frederick, Back Westgate

Coal Dealers.
Coulson William, Southgate
Langley Frederick, Southgate
N.E. Railway Co.— W. Train, agent
Train Geo. Ed., (and lime and gravel agent), Southgate

Corn & Flour Dealers.
Hall & Son, Southgate
Hobson John, Southgate
Huntsman Seth (and carter), Back Westgate

Cowkeepers.
Bingham Joshua, Hornsea Burton
Hansom Benj., Seaton road
Harker John C. (and livery stbls.), White hs., Southgate
Robinson Thomas, Lelley lane

Drapers (Linen and Woollen).
Drinkrow Robert Stephenson (& millinor & gentlemen's mercer), Market place and Newbegin
Fisher Richard Gibson (and general outfitter and agent for P. & P. Campbell's Dye works, Perth), Market place
Foster Walter (baby linen), Newbegin; h Hull
Johnson William (and tailor), Southgate
Laking Cook (and stationer and bookseller), Newbegin
Pearson William R. (and millinery, fancy goods and carpet warehs.), Newbegin

Dressmakers.
Anthony Miss Jane, Newbegin
Atkinson Miss Frances J., Southgate
Carr Mrs. Lucy, Newbegin
Drinkrow R. S., Market place
Dunn Miss Emma, Newbegin
Garton Mrs. Annie, Southgate
Granger Miss Lucy, Southgate
Grantham Miss Christiana Newbegin
Leeson Miss Eliz., Southgate
Peers Miss Amelia S., South'g'te
Pickering Mrs. Lucy, Southgate
Stones Arthur (and fancy goods dlr. & photogphr.), Southgate

Farmers.
Ake Henry, Southorpe grange
Bateson Harry Taylor, Old hall
Bell Robert; h Atwick
Bulson John, Southgate
Feaster Frederick Dennison, Brockholme
Grainger Jos. John (at Seaton), Newbegin
Harrison Mrs. Emma, Southgate
Heslop Geo., Southorpe farm
Holmes Jas., Bowholme lane
Hornsey Mrs. Ann, Trinity House farm (& Beverley & Pexton farms), Hornsea Burton

HOUSE of TOWNEND
Established 1906 · Wine Merchants

HORNSEA'S LOCAL WINE MERCHANT

* WIDEST RANGE OF WINES IN THE AREA

* BEERS AT COMPETITIVE PRICES

* MALT WHISKY SPECIALIST

* FRIENDLY KNOWLEDGEABLE STAFF

**HOUSE OF TOWNEND
55 NEWBEGIN
HORNSEA**

TEL: 0964 532353

OPEN 10 am - 10 pm   MONDAY TO SATURDAY

Pets and Gardens
53 Newbegin, Hornsea

Everything your pets need

Your garden will look a picture if you use our seeds, compost, fertilisers, weed and insect killers, tools and plants

Freshly cut flowers to beautify your home or as a gift for others

Free delivery service

Telephone 532323

Proprietor: CHERYL JEBSON

2 — Seaside Resort?

It has been said of the census returns that they give a snapshot of a community at one moment in time. If this is true, it might be said of Hornsea that, at the very least, the picture is somewhat blurred; one would be hard put to it, for example, to divine from the 1891 return that Hornsea was a seaside resort. There is mention of only five inns and hotels, only one of which had any guests on the day of the census. There are two refreshment-house keepers, one boat builder (but no hirer of boats or pleasure vessels) and just over a dozen lodging-house keepers with no more than a handful of boarders all told, all single working men. It is not the picture of what was described at the time as a popular resort.

One explanation is, of course, the timing of the census. The day was deliberately chosen to find as many people as possible in their normal place of residence, and Monday morning, 6 April 1891, was not a time when many people in England were holidaying. Another reason the Hornsea census return does not seem to give a true picture of the town's activities is that for many residents the holiday trade was very much a part-time affair, and their connections with it were not indicated in the return. To find a truer picture we have to supplement our snapshot with other records of the time. If we turn to the trade directories, for example, we find well over 50 Hornsea residents advertising as lodging-house keepers. In the census return these people are recorded as having occupations such as shopkeepers, craftsmen, labourers, small farmers, gardeners and charwomen, in addition to the few who actually described themselves as lodging-house keepers.

The visitors lists printed in *The Hornsea Gazette* give another aspect of the story — the proprietor of a boarding house is nearly always the wife in the household, and in the census return a wife's occupation is very rarely stated. A woman's occupation is only given if she is the head of the household (i.e. widowed or single) or if she is a daughter and has a job, or if she is a servant in the house.

The census return, therefore, is not a good indicator of the people involved in the holiday trade. The visitors lists give a better picture, at least of the number of people taking in visitors and the number of houses being rented to holiday-makers. In the August Bank Holiday week of 1887, there were about 400 visitors staying in Hornsea. About 40 of them were accommodated at the five hotels; the others were at the 50 or so boarding houses or staying in rented houses or cottages, of which there were about 20. An indication of the class of these visitors is given by the fact that practically all those taking rented accommodation were accompanied by their servants. The list included nine ministers of religion, two captains and a doctor. About three-quarters of the visitors came from Hull and other places in the East Riding, but there were people from the West Riding, London, Newcastle, Birmingham, Wolverhampton, Edinburgh, Essex and Dorset. Mrs. Hall, who was staying at Mere Cottage, came from Brooklyn, U.S.A.

Set against the permanent population of 2,000, the majority of whom had little to do with the holiday trade, the number of visitors is quite large, and must have added greatly to the prosperity of the town. Besides those who provided accommodation, others to benefit were the shopkeepers and provision merchants, the chemists and druggists catering for the health-conscious and hypochondriacal, the proprietors of bathing machines, the cab proprietors and the cowkeepers with the extra customers for their milk. In an age of middle-class piety, no doubt the churches and chapels also benefited. It is perhaps significant that the churchwardens of St. Nicholas decided in 1891 that, as church seats became free when people moved from the parish, they should no longer be appropriated to any particular person but should be labelled 'Free and unappropriated'. Visitors were welcome!

What was there to attract the visitors, many of whom came for stays of a month or more? They could go bathing in the sea, of course. In the nineties mixed bathing was only just becoming permissible, thanks to the introduction of bathing costumes. Previous to that, the men usually swam naked, and the women were immersed, clothed in a gown, from the shelter of a bathing machine. A Hornsea bye-law, proposed in 1864 by Joseph Armytage Wade, required male and female bathers to take their dips from bathing machines separated from each other by a distance of at least 200 yards. It was Joseph Wade who had had a pier built at Hornsea. It was a long-drawn-out project, which began in 1866 and did not achieve its aim until 1880. Alas, it was an amenity which was no longer available to the visitor of the 1890s, for in the very same year that the pier was built it was damaged beyond repair when the ship, the Earl of Derby, was dashed against the end in a violent storm. Still, visitors could always stroll along the promenade, which in those days was a broad gravel path along the cliff top, or sit in one of the shelters, viewing the sea and the flower beds. There might be a concert or dancing in the Public Rooms in Newbegin (on the site of the present public library) or a musical promenade in the grounds of the Alexandra Hotel. For the energetic there was rowing on the Mere or tennis on the courts close by the Mere. Fishing in the Mere was restricted to those who were prepared to pay £5 5s (£5.25) for an annual licence. *Fretwell's Guide to Hornsea* of 1894 recommends many walks around the town, including a six-mile stroll along the cliffs to Aldbrough. One could also drive out to Burton Constable and view the house and grounds. There were interesting local churches to be visited. And for

Hornsea's gravel promenade, looking south to the Marine Hotel. The promenade was laid out in 1891. Note the bathing machines on the beach in front of the hotel. The promenade was almost completely washed away in a great storm of 1906, an event which prompted the building of the concrete sea-wall and promenade.

Donkeys on the sands below the remains of Hornsea pier. Donkey-driving was a source of employment for Hornsea schoolboys and a cause for truancy.

the botanist, the geologist and the fresh-water biologist there was a wealth of flora, clays exposed in the cliffs, and mollusca in the Mere to be studied.

Whatever the attractions, the fact was that many people returned each year for the season. Some eventually came to settle in Hornsea. William Schultetus, the German consul from Hull, was staying in Football Green in 1887. In 1891 he was a resident of Hornsea and living at No. 1 Alexandra Terrace with his Hull-born wife, two sons and two servants. In 1869 George Haller, of the ship-owning firm of Earle and Haller in Hull, had taken sufficient liking to Hornsea to contribute £25 towards the proposed new Wesleyan chapel in Newbegin. Two years later he was in residence in Hornsea and in 1891 was living at No. 2 Carlton Terrace with his family and one servant. There is an interesting story about the Liggins family — father, mother and three daughters — who were staying at No. 10 Wilton Terrace in 1887. They returned there many times and eventually built a house on the plot at the end of the terrace for their own accommodation. One of the daughters was a pianist of considerable talent and, in order to promote her public image, changed her name to Ligginska, a move, apparently, which proved of some benefit.

There were not many families who could afford to spend the full season at Hornsea. Very few workers received a full week off at August Bank Holiday time or, indeed, at any time of the year. For the majority of working folk, August Monday was the sum total of their summer holiday. By the 1890s, however, many working men were earning enough to afford a day out with their families at a nearby resort, and the North Eastern Railway frequently laid on cheap day trips to Hornsea from Hull to cater for them. Not for them, however, was Hornsea's attraction the stratification of the cliffs, or even the mollusca abounding in the Mere. Their recreation lay mostly on the sands — a paddle in the sea, and sand-castles and donkey rides

Usher's Refreshment Saloon advertised in Fretwell's Guide to Hornsea, *1894.*

G. USHER'S
Refreshment Saloon
The SANDS, Hornsea.

The above Saloon having now been enlarged is replete for accommodating Schools, large Parties, etc., at reasonable charges. Terms on application.

	s	d
First-Class Tea (with Ham)	1	0
Plain Tea	0	8
Children's Tea	0	6
Cup of Tea	0	1
Cup of Coffee	0	1
Hot Water	0	2
,, Children	0	1

Communications by Post will receive prompt attention.

for the kids. (Many a Hornsea schoolboy played truant in order to earn a few coppers donkey-driving.) On the sands was Usher's refreshment saloon, with a first-class ham tea for a shilling (5p), and a cup of tea or coffee for a penny (0.4p). And it was on the sands where the pierrots and Punch-and-Judy man provided their entertainments.

There were other entertainments. At peak seasons events were organized to attract both visitors and locals to the beach area. Up to the end of the eighties there had been horse-racing on the sands. In July 1885, special trains were run from Hull for a meeting which took place before several thousand spectators. There were five races with a total prize-money of £50. The finishing post was opposite the Marine Hotel, and the slopes on either side of the hotel formed the grandstand. The start of racing that year had to be put back from the advertised time of 1.30 p.m. to 3.00 p.m. because of the tide. Races were from half a mile to a mile and a quarter in length. It was a fine day but, as reported in the *Hull Times,* the meeting was marred by a minor riot: 'The pony race created great dissatisfaction among the spectators by the running of Mr. Jones' Nellie. The horse would have won easily but, within only a few yards of the post, it was deliberately pulled in, and Mr. Flanders' Maggie won by a head. The jockey's conduct caused much indignation and he had a very warm reception on returning to the weigh-in. He was pelted with stones and other missiles and loudly hooted and, but for his timely escape to the committee tent, he would no doubt have been roughly used. The officials and police had considerable difficulty in preventing the crowd taking the tent by storm, and it was some time before the excitement subsided.' Perhaps it was scenes like these that brought an end to horse-racing in Hornsea.

The Hornsea Regatta was less prone to disturbance (for one thing, the spectators could not get at the competitors so easily). It was first held in 1876 and was still being held on August Bank Holidays in the nineties. Amongst the participants were fishermen who had come up the coast from Sheringham in Norfolk to meet the herring shoals moving south. At sea there were races for yachts, cobles, rowing boats, punts and tubs. There was also a water-polo match. On shore there were donkey races, sack races, and obstacle races for men and children, as well as a tug o' war.

Sunday School excursions and trips organized by other bodies brought smaller groups to the sands. Photographs of the day show farm carts, laden with children, being pulled by horses or, sometimes, steam traction engines. One wonders how the 'best frocks' fared from the smuts emitted by the engines. From the photographs it does appear that the children were enjoying themselves and it really was a Sunday School treat. The same cannot always be said of the adults, who no doubt breathed a sigh of relief when they got all their charges back home. Sunday School treats were a double bonus for the children because they took place during the school term, and the children were given a holiday for the day. Many of the Hornsea pupils played truant to be on the sands when children from other villages or from Hull came on their outings to Hornsea. Hornsea children, of course, went elsewhere for their treats, the 'Band of Hope', for example, going to Bridlington in 1890. Up to 1891, the summer holidays for Hornsea pupils began about the middle of August to allow the children to help with the harvest but, beginning in 1892, the school managers brought the start of the holiday forward by about three weeks. As the master wrote in the school log on 31 July 1893 when the school broke up: 'It was proved last year that visitors to Hornsea took away more children than the Harvest. We shall also miss 2 weeks of exceptionally bad attendance viz. the Regatta and the Wesleyan Anniversary weeks'. The master of the school, at least, was beginning to look on Hornsea more as a seaside resort than an agricultural village.

But becoming a resort was not what every resident of Hornsea wanted. It was all right attracting the kind of visitor who desired nothing more than to contemplate the churning ocean or minutely inspect the boulder clay of Hornsea's cliffs, but it was a different matter encouraging the type whose interest in boulder clay extended no further than selecting the larger fragments of it to hurl at the jockey who had just pulled the favourite in the 3.30. Hornsea probably began resisting day-trippers almost as soon as the railway began offering them cheap excursions to the coast. Perhaps the reason was that some of the wealthy people who came to reside in Hornsea also played a part in the government of the town. Men like Thomas Holmes, Christopher Pickering and Alfred Maw, Hull businessmen residing in Hornsea, all served on Hornsea's local governing bodies in the 1890s. As men who no doubt looked on Hornsea as a quiet retreat from the hurly-burly of Hull, they would tend to promote the interests of the residents rather than those of the day-trippers. Hornsea's reputation for its 'quiet and subdued air' was probably already well established by the 1890s. It is a reputation which continues to persist.

Beach scene at Hornsea in the early part of this century. The building in the centre of the photograph had been the entrance to the pier, completed in 1880 and wrecked the same year. The swing-boats were part of the attraction of the beach for the day-trippers.

THE VERNON GALLERY

Needlework/Picture Framing
Posters, Cards
and Prints
Extensive Art and Craft Section
Gifts

136-138 Newbegin, Hornsea
Tel: 532986

*Quality Hairdesign
by Professionals*

126 Newbegin, Hornsea
Tel: (0964) 532484

CLASSIC FOOTWEAR

For all your family's footwear
at highest quality
and lowest prices

 Brevitt

MARKET PLACE, HORNSEA
Tel: (0964) 533486

E.G. COULSON BUILDERS

*FOR ALL YOUR BUILDING NEEDS
ROUND HORNSEA
you should consult*
E. G. COULSON (BUILDER) LTD
76 Newbegin, Hornsea, HU18 1AD
Tel: (0964) 533206 & 532015

3 — Residential Town

Hornsea has a history as a market centre and an agricultural village going back several centuries. In the early part of the 19th century it was also gaining a reputation as a resort with a reasonable climate, and was considered very healthy. It had many things to recommend it to visitors. Initially, it was the spa, or mineral spring, near the north-east corner of the Mere, which had attracted the health-conscious for a fortnight's stay or more each year. Later, as sea-bathing became more popular, it was the broad, flat sands which proved the attraction. To these could be added the attractions of the Public Rooms where dances, concerts and other functions were held, the annual regatta and other social events, and the pier (albeit, very short-lived). In the early part of 1891, a gravel promenade was laid out on the North Cliff. Above all, there was the ease with which Hornsea could be reached via the railway.

The coming of the Hull and Hornsea railway in 1864 had also resulted in many professional and businessmen coming to live in Hornsea and commuting to Hull. For them the attractions were no doubt the scenery and the sea air, but also the very practical ones of water on tap and proper sewage disposal, both of which had been provided by the end of the 1870s. In these last two respects, Hornsea had the advantage over the old-established residential areas to the west of Hull — places such as Anlaby, Hessle, Ferriby and Kirk Ella, which were still relying on springs, wells and earth closets. Another amenity, domestic lighting by gas, had become available in Hornsea in 1866. By 1891, Hornsea was

Residential Hornsea: houses in New Road. The first house was, and still is, Oriel House. In 1891 it was occupied by William Dyson, a Hull coal merchant, and his family and servants. The remainder of the row was Grosvenor Terrace, numbered 1 to 15 (now numbered 3 to 31, odd numbers only). The darker building in the centre was Nos. 7 and 8, Mary Skinner's High School for Girls. Two of the houses in the terrace were unoccupied, one was a lodging house, six were occupied by retired people, and the remaining four by a wholesale grocer, a shipyard manager, a timber merchant and the minister of the Hornsea Wesleyan Circuit.

Wilton Terrace, two rows of double-fronted houses at right angles to each other, conveniently close to the railway station for the Hull commuters. The houses were numbered 1 to 10 from the right, as they are today. Only half of No. 1 is showing in the photograph. Number 4 is the corner house which faces in two directions. The three-storied house is No. 7. Living at Nos. 1 to 4 in 1891 were, respectively, a ship-owner's manager, a mineral-water engineer, an architect and a merchant's clerk. Number 5 was a lodging house. At No. 6 was a solicitor, at No. 7 was a wholesale druggist, and No. 8 was a lodging house. Number 9, just in the photograph, and No. 10 were unoccupied and may have been used as holiday accommodation.

Alexandra Terrace, Railway Street. Another terrace of houses close to the railway station. In 1891 they were the homes of a German consul, a seed merchant, a corn-merchant's clerk and a stockbroker. All four men probably worked in Hull and one can imagine them setting out from these houses for their offices each week-day morning to catch the train for Hull.

Christopher Pickering, Hull trawler-owner and benefactor of both Hull and Hornsea. He played a leading part in the affairs of Hornsea. In 1891 he lived at Holme Lea in Eastgate but later moved to nearby Hornsea House when the previous owner, Joseph Armytage Wade, died in 1896. Both houses were some distance from the holiday hubbub of the railway station.

houses had been built close to the railway station and more were in the course of construction. Wilton Terrace, within a stone's throw of the station, was typical of such development. Of the eight inhabited houses in the terrace in 1891, one was occupied by a works' manager, one by an engineer, one by an architect, one by a merchant's clerk, one by a solicitor and one by a wholesale druggist. The other two were lodging houses.

Wealthier businessmen chose to live further away from the station with its summer-time hurly-burly of the day-trippers. One such businessman was Joseph Armytage Wade, a Hornsea man, who lived at Hornsea House in Eastgate. He is described in the census return as 'Timber Merchant, Farmer, Engineer, J.P.'. His business interests were in both Hull and Hornsea. His timber business was in Hull; his farmland was in and around Hornsea; his brick and tile works were in Hornsea, near Hornsea Bridge, but there was also part of this business in Hull; near the works in Hornsea was the hydraulic-pump works in which Wade was a partner. Wade had been instrumental in bringing the railway to Hornsea and was also chairman of the company which built the ill-fated pier, completed in 1880 and damaged beyond repair in the same year. Wade was actively connected with the Liberal Party, being president of the Hornsea and District Liberal Club. His daughter, Harriet, married Samuel Plimsoll, a former Liberal M.P., known as the Sailor's Friend for his Bill against the overloading of ships and the consequent introduction of the Plimsoll Line.

Another resident in Eastgate was Christopher Pickering, the Hull trawler-owner and benefactor to both Hornsea and his home town of Hull. To Hull he donated the land for Pickering Park and the nearby almshouses. In Hornsea he provided the almshouses which stand in Newbegin. Both Hull and Hornsea have thoroughfares named after him.

Thomas Barton Holmes, head of the Hull tanning firm, lived at Elim Lodge in Cliff Road. He was

becoming increasingly popular as a residential town. The census shows the town's population to have been made up of 425 households and, of these, about 50 could be described as having as the breadwinner someone whose job was probably in Hull — clerical workers, business men and professional people.

To accommodate the commuters, a number of

Cliff Road (Elim Lodge)	1	Thomas B. Holmes	Head	M	55	Farmer J.P. C.C.
		Sarah do	Wife	M	50	
		George F. do	Son	S	29	Farmer
		Ethel do	Daur	S	23	
		Ruth A. do	do	S	21	
		Kathleen do	do	S	19	
		Margaret A.C. do	do		13	Scholar
		Harold C. do	Son		10	do
		Samuel Lord	Visitor	M	66	Wesleyan Minister
		Elizabeth A. do	Visitor	M	58	
		Mary Longmate	Serv	S	29	Cook domestic serv.
		Eliza Garton	do	S	25	Sewing maid do
		Ellen Clements	do	S	29	Waiting maid do
		Sarah A. Crawforth	do	S	24	Housemaid do
		Emily Jackson	do	S	17	Kitchen maid do

The occupants of Elim Lodge on census day, 1891. Thomas Barton Holmes, head of the Hull tanning firm, Justice of the Peace and County Councillor, is the head of the family. Besides members of the family, there were six servants and a visiting Wesleyan Minister and his wife in the house on the morning of 6 April.

particularly interested in education. An energetic member of the Hull School Board and a prime mover in the introduction of technical education in Hull, he also served on the Hornsea School Board.

At Oriel House, next to the Congregational church, in New Road, lived William Dyson, a Hull coal merchant. At the opposite end of the terrace of houses, at Grosvenor Lodge, was Alfred Maw, partner in the Hull furniture makers of Maw, Till, Kirke and Co. Other Hull businessmen living in Hornsea were George Haller, of Earle and Haller, shipowners, John Henson, solicitor, Arthur Anderton, general merchant in Hull's High Street, Thomas Gregson of Stuart and Gregson, bagging manufacturers, William Gibson of Gibson Brothers, paint and varnish manufacturers, Peter Gaskell, architect, Thomas Redfern, solicitor, Walter Whiteside, stockbroker, and William Field, seed crusher.

Many of these men took an active part in the affairs of Hornsea. Wade, besides his involvement with the railway and the pier, was also a key figure in the establishment of Hornsea's Local Board of Health, chairman of the Hornsea Gas Light and Coke Co. and churchwarden of St. Nicholas till his resignation in 1883. In 1892, at the age of well over 70 he was still chairman of the School Board and one of the feoffees of the church lands. Wade's involvement in Hornsea's development was probably one of self-interest since, even before the railway came, he owned quite an amount of land in the area, not to mention the brickworks which benefited from the subsequent building activity which followed on the opening of the railway.

The interest of the others was probably more one of paternalism combined with the Victorian ideal of the wealthy taking on public responsibilities. As already mentioned, Thomas Holmes, an active educationalist, was on the Hornsea School Board. He was also chairman of the Local Board of Health and, when its role was taken over by the Urban District Council in 1895, chairman of that. He was a leading member of the Hornsea Wesleyans, as was George Haller. Christopher Pickering was a member of Hornsea's Urban District Council. William Dyson was on the School Board. Alfred Maw was a churchwarden of St. Nicholas, on the Local Board of Health and then on the Urban District Council. Maw's Victorian paternalism as an employer is shown by his giving his Hull employees a half-day holiday in 1891 and conveying them to Hornsea to watch a cricket match between a team of his employees and the Hornsea club. He then treated both teams to a tea at the Mere Hotel (now the Alexandra). In 1897 Maw and his wife presented all the children of Hornsea with Jubilee mugs and medals on the occasion of Queen Victoria's Diamond Jubilee.

Men like these, with wealth and position, must have had considerable influence on the way the town developed. As men who had come to Hornsea as a pleasant place to live, any policies they helped to form must have been more with the interest of the residents at heart than for the benefit of the day-trippers and the holiday trade. It was an attitude which persisted, and Hornsea has long considered itself as a town by the sea rather than a seaside resort.

Elim Lodge, in 1891 the home of T. B. Holmes and his family. The house is now a nursing home.

Brian Scaife
Quality Butcher

31 Market Place, Hornsea

Tel: (0964) 533141

MARKET PLACE PHARMACY

FREE PRESCRIPTION DELIVERY SERVICE

Full range of medicines
Homoeopathic products
and Herbal remedies

Andrew J. Snee
Your local Hornsea Chemist

Telephone: 532967

DAVID TIERNAN
I.B.I.C.C.

2 MARKET PLACE
HORNSEA

Telephone:
533221
Home;
534316

JOINERY & BUILDING CONTRACTOR

Specialists in Restoration and Roofing Work

Levels of Hornsea

THE STORE THAT OFFERS YOU MORE

* Gifts * Fashion Accessories and Hosiery
* Greeting cards * Kitchenware * Bedding
* Handicrafts and Dressmaking * Furniture
* Baby Clothes and Gifts

Eight fully stocked departments all year round and a fantastic Christmas Department from September

Also next door -- Level Two
for all your flower arranging
and gardening needs

Monday-Saturday, 9.00-5.30

FREE CUSTOMER CAR PARKING

**16 & 14b Market Place
Hornsea**
0964 534079/536338

JOHN ATKINSON BDS

Dental Surgeon

**9 CLIFF ROAD, HORNSEA
Tel: 533293**

NHS or private treatment available

Surgery hours:
Mon-Fri: 9.00-12.30; 2.00-5.30
and Sat: 9.00-12 noon

Pizzeria Restaurant  For a casual night out!

Luigi's

Restaurant
Broadway, Hornsea. Tel: 533101

Dinner dances, Weddings, Private parties and all special occasions

---

Walkers Stores

For your every need
including groceries, fruit, vegetables
bread and cakes
wines and spirits
High class butchers

**4 The Greenway, Hornsea
Tel: 532584**

WOODS OF HORNSEA

BUILDERS MERCHANTS
PLANT AND TOOL HIRE
TIMBER SUPPLIES

Old Bridge Road, Hornsea
North Humberside, HU18 1RP
Telephone: 0964 534664
Fax; 0964 536418

D.I.Y./PLANT AND TOOL HIRE

The biggest and best selection!

Easy parking and FREE delivery
Open Mon-Sat, 8.00 am - 5 pm

4 — The Southgate Area in 1891

Hornsea was a village that grew up round the Mere. The old houses and streets curved round the east end of the lake, with only two streets, Eastgate and Newbegin, extending towards the sea. In the Middle Ages the little port of Hornsea Beck had been established at the cliff edge but this had disappeared, due to erosion, by the early 17th century. At the beginning of the 19th century most Hornsea people, including the fishing families, lived closer to the Mere than to the sea, and Hornsea's streets consisted of only Southgate, Back Southgate, the Mere Side, Market Place, Newbegin, Westgate, Back Westgate and Eastgate.

As Hornsea began to develop as a seaside resort and residential town, more streets and buildings came into being to the east of the town. The Marine Hotel was built close to the cliff edge in 1837, and New Road was laid out in 1848. When the Hull and Hornsea Railway was completed in 1864 the terminus was near the beach, and many new houses, especially those of Hull commuters, were built in streets laid out between the east end of Newbegin and the railway terminus. This became the fashionable area of the town, and the old part of the town became more the working-class area. When John Barr, the enumerator for the southern half of Hornsea in the 1891 census, began distributing the schedules in Southgate he must have reflected on how the area had changed since he had been a lad in Hornsea more than 40 years before. Then, it had been considered to be

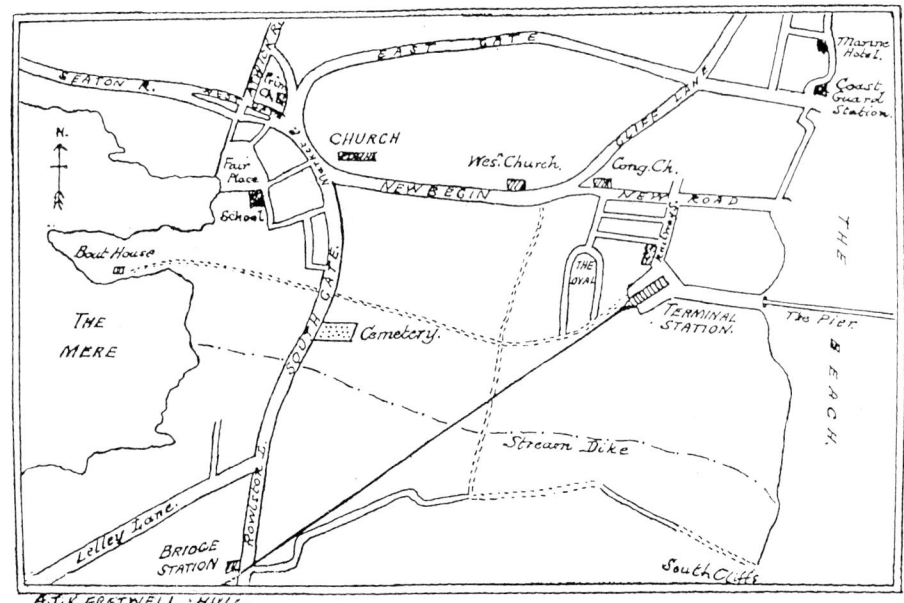

Outline sketch of Hornsea from Fretwell's Guide of 1894. The new development lies between the east end of Newbegin and the railway station. The area shown as the Oval is now Eastbourne Road and Burton Road. Both the Wesleyan and Congregational churches had been rebuilt close to the new development.

Shops on the west side of Southgate at the turn of the century. They have a decidedly run-down appearance.

quite stylish. The Congregationalists had had their chapel there, the Wesleyan chapel had been in Back Southgate, and the ministers for both denominations had lived in Southgate. Since those days, both chapels had been rebuilt in the newer part of the town where the ministers now lived. Speculative development along Southgate had resulted in the building of many two-up-and-two-down houses, such as those in Ocean Terrace and Welbourne Terrace. The older buildings and houses, many constructed of cobblestones taken from the beach, had a distinctly run-down air about them. As John Barr gave out the census schedules he may have mused on the crampedness of most of the dwellings in Southgate compared with the spaciousness of the more modern houses he had visited in New Road and around the railway station.

After collecting the schedules, transferring the information to his return, and forwarding it to Beverley, John Barr no doubt quickly forgot about the statistics he had so carefully copied out. It has been left to us today to analyse some of the information on his census return. For the purpose of this brief survey the study has been confined to the area between the Mere and the west side of Southgate. It includes the houses along the west side of Southgate itself, the houses in Back Southgate and Welbourne Terrace, and two houses in Mereside (the other houses in Mereside were dealt with by the other enumerator covering the north side of Hornsea). In all, the area contained 63 occupied houses. In addition, there were eight places described as 'Uninhabited' although, besides empty houses, these could have included premises such as lock-up shops or the old Wesleyan chapel which at that time was being used as the headquarters of the Hornsea and District Liberal Club. Except for Welbourne Terrace and some cottages which stood nearby, most of the properties are still standing.

As part of a town which had expanded rapidly over

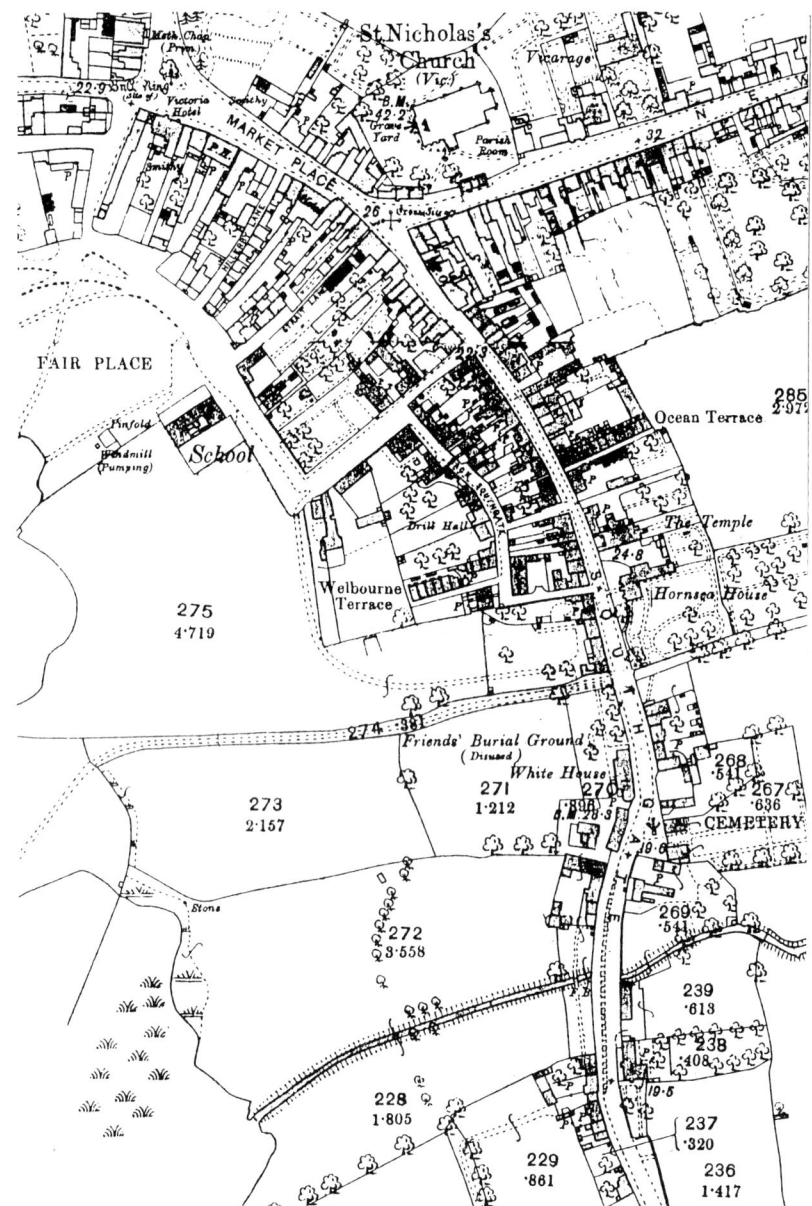

The area between Southgate and the Mere in 1891. The building outlines clearly include the 'out offices' of Welbourne Terrace. Just to the east of Welbourne Terrace is a row of two-roomed cottages one of which housed a family of eight. Note the pumps, marked 'P', in the yards of some of the houses. (Reproduction from the 1891 Ordnance Survey map.)

The former Wesleyan Methodist chapel in Back Southgate. In 1891 it was the headquarters of the Hornsea and District Liberal Club. The new chapel had been built in 1870 in a better-class area at the east end of Newbegin.

the previous 25 years, the area had many people who originated from outside Hornsea — men and women who had been attracted to a centre of some development. Of the 139 people aged 21 and over, only 33 (24%) were born in Hornsea. Seventy-seven (55%) came from elsewhere in the East Riding, six came from the North and West Ridings and seven from Lincolnshire. Sixteen (11.5%) were born elsewhere in Britain, including Hampshire, Surrey, Cornwall, Suffolk, Surrey, Warwickshire, Bedfordshire, Liverpool and Scotland. Though somewhat remote, Hornsea's position on part of Britain's great rail network made it accessible to people from all over the country.

Of the 63 heads of households, only eight described themselves as employers of labour. One was fisherman (and boat-owner) George Usher, and five were small shopkeepers or artisans. In the cases of Frederick Carter, grocer, and William Robinson and Thomas Arksey, both shoemakers, their work force may have been no more than the teen-age apprentices they employed. In the cases of Robinson and Arksey, these were their own sons or other relatives. In all, 15 householders were neither employers of labour nor employees (today we would call them self-employed). They included small shopkeepers, two fishermen, two cowkeepers, a hawker, a miller, a blacksmith and a bricklayer. Four householders lived on their own means. The remainder were employed in a great variety of occupations. Eleven of the householders were women, mostly widows. These included three of those living on their own means. Of the others, one ran a dame school, two were dressmakers, two were charwomen, one was a laundress, one a nurse and one combined her occupation of seamstress with teaching.

In an age of large families and people taking in lodgers, it might be expected that there were plenty of others living in the area, besides the heads of the households, who had wage-earning occupations of some kind or other. However, on the whole, the houses were small, and very few children appear to have stayed on with their families after they left school. Some single daughters continued to live with elderly or widowed parents, often earning money as

White House, Southgate — the name it was given on the Ordnance Survey map of 1891. In the census return it is called the 'late Old Hotel'. It had changed from being an inn to being a temperance hotel in 1875. In 1891 it was occupied by John Clappison Harker, described as a cowkeeper in the census, but who was also advertising apartments at the time and, as the photograph shows, running a livery stable.

dressmakers, but it seems to have been rare for the children of the area to stay with their families beyond the age of 15. As we have seen, tradesmen, like William Robinson and Thomas Arksey, employed their sons as apprentices, but there were not many families like those of Thomas Peers, a painter in Southgate, where there were ten children up to the age of 19 still living at home. Here the two eldest, both girls, were employed as laundresses. George Keith, a labourer living in Southgate, and his wife had seven children living at home. The eldest, a 16-year-old girl, had a job as a servant, and the 14-year-old was an errand boy. But these two families were exceptions.

Neither was this the sort of Victorian middle-class area where servants were employed in the household. Three of the shopkeepers in Southgate each had a 14- to 16-year-old living-in on the premises as a servant, either to help in the shop or give a hand with the housework. The only other house where a servant lived-in was the White House in Southgate. Here, John Harker, a cowkeeper, who also advertised apartments, employed 16-year-old Annie Robinson to help his wife with their four children and any lodgers they might have (there was none on census day). Only three other houses in the area were advertising board and lodgings in *Bulmer's Directory* of 1892, and only two of these had lodgers on census day. Joseph Everingham, one of the ministers on the Hornsea Primitive Methodist circuit, was staying in Back Southgate at The Elms, the home of John Witty, a cowkeeper and Primitive Methodist lay preacher. William Moore, a hired preacher, lodged on Mere Side at the house of William Bassindale, corn miller and also a Primitive Methodist lay preacher. On census day six other households, not advertising in *Bulmer's Directory*, each had a working lodger. Taking into account all the working population — householders, relatives, servants, apprentices and lodgers — the breakdown of occupations, firstly for men, is as follows:

Agricultural and general labourers	16
Building, plumbing, painting, joinery	10
Shopkeepers and assistants	23
Fishermen	4
Railway employees	2
Other occupations	17

Joinery workers were not necessarily all concerned in building; some may have been engaged in repairs to carriages, farm vehicles and implements of husbandry. Many of the shopkeepers, such as shoemakers, tailors, watchmaker and saddler, made the things they sold. The men in the other occupations included two preachers, two cowkeepers, a coalman, a cartman, two gardeners and a market gardener, a hawker, a blacksmith (who would have been employed either at one of the smithies in Market Place or at Wade and Cherry's engineering works near Hornsea Bridge railway station), a miller, a clerk, a policeman, a steam-engine fitter and a stationary-engine driver (these two were probably in charge of machinery at Wade and Cherry's) and the Battery Sergeant Major at the East Yorkshire Volunteers' drill hall in Back Southgate.

For women the breakdown of occupations is as follows:

Dressmakers	12
Laundresses	4
Charwomen	3
Domestic servants	6
Other occupations	11

The women in the other occupations included three housekeepers, two nurses, a companion, a schoolmistress, a seamstress cum schoolmistress, a draper's assistant, a telegraph clerk and a confectioner. No doubt the orders for dressmaking came from the more well-to-do sector of the town.

Very few wives were credited with occupations in the census. Some of the dressmakers were married, and Bessie Norman, described as a confectioner, was the wife of a confectioner, but the other wage-earning women were either widows or unmarried. In the 63 households in the area there were 43 housewives with no wage-earning occupation given in the census. Together with the children they helped to make the non-earners the larger proportion of the population.

There were 96 school children (listed as scholars in the census) and 39 below school age. Three teen-age girls were listed as 'At home', that is, they were helping with the family. Housewives and non-working children thus totalled 181 out of the 302 people living in the area: 60% of the population were dependent on a breadwinner.

The list of occupations shows the area between Southgate and the Mere to have been largely working class, and many of the houses were quite small. Of the 63 occupied dwellings, 26 had only four rooms and one had only three rooms. In Back Southgate there was a row of three two-roomed cottages, in one of which lived 46-year-old widow Anne Wright with her seven children aged from one to 16. Anne was a charwoman, and 16-year-old Gertrude was 'At home'. Other homes in the area were almost as crowded. Welbourne Terrace consisted of a row of six two-up-and-two-down houses. On census day one house in the row was unoccupied. Families of four or five lived in four of the houses but, at No. 1, plumber George Evans lived with his wife and seven children. Thomas Arksey, the shoemaker, lived in a four-roomed house in Back Southgate with his wife, two young sons, his 20-year-old daughter, who was in domestic service, and his teen-age son and nephew, who were his apprentices. He also managed to accommodate a lodger. By the standards of the present day, conditions may have been a bit crowded, but far worse conditions prevailed in the slums of some of the big cities.

With the problem of overcrowding, there was also the problem of sanitation. It is probably true to say that in the 1890s all the houses in the Southgate area were served by either earth closets or cesspits, considered even in those days as sources of infection, at least by the school medical officer, as the following entry in the school log book shows:

'Jan. 3rd 1896. Gave a Holiday this aftn. as there are so many away ill. Dr. Johns informs me that Scarlet Fever is in Welbourne Terrace & that none of the children in that Terrace ought to come to school. He says that the out offices in that Terrace are in an extremely unsanitary condition.'

However, regarding sanitary arrangements, the Southgate area was not much different from most of the old part of Hornsea. (It was not until some years later that the Hornsea Urban District Council considered it necessary to pass a bye-law forbidding the display of toilet basins in plumbers' shop windows.)

Piped water was laid on to the area from the Leys Hill waterworks but not every owner or landlord could or would afford to have it piped into the house. For the occupants it meant a trip to one of the public stand pipes in Market Place or Southgate to collect fresh water. In the 1890s some of the properties still had pumps dating back to the days before the opening of the waterworks in 1879. These pumps took their water from shallow wells, which were always liable to contamination from nearby cesspits, and hence were possible sources of infection. The Ordnance Survey map of 1891 shows about half a dozen pumps still in existence between Southgate and the Mere. The position of one suggests that it had originally served the houses in Welbourne Terrace and the nearby cottages. Others were in the backyards of shops in Southgate and there was one in the yard of White House. The water from the pumps was far softer than the water from Leys Hill, and it is probably no coincidence that there was still a pump at the house three doors away from White House, where Elizabeth Walker and her two daughters ran a laundry.

Despite a few smells, some overcrowding and the risk of enteric infection, the area could in no way be considered benighted. Southgate probably provided the bulk of the large congregations that attended the Primitive Methodist chapel in nearby Market Place. Besides the two preachers lodging in the area, there were eight prominent members of the local Primitives living there. Lay preachers William Bassindale and John Witty have already been mentioned. Other lay preachers included Thomas Arksey and William Robinson, the two shoemakers, and James Meyers, a gardener. Also living in the area were the steward of the Hornsea chapel, an exhorter and one of the trustees — one a tailor, one a labourer and one a fisherman. It is perhaps also significant that there were few public houses near Southgate. There were three in Market Place, but no more than when Hornsea's population had been far less. In fact, the White House in Southgate, which had been a public house for the first three-quarters of the century, had been converted into a temperance hotel in 1875 and had remained as such until 1885. In 1891 it was occupied by John Harker who, besides keeping cows and letting apartments, ran livery stables from the premises. On the opposite side of Southgate, the former Congregational chapel had been taken over by a temperance organization known as the Good Templars which, at least until as late as 1888, was providing tea and entertainment on the premises. Southgate may have been the poorer part of Hornsea, but it was Godly. Whether this was the conclusion which the enumerator, John Barr, came to is another matter!

HORNSEA POTTERY, PAST AND PRESENT
1949 - 1993

MANUFACTURERS OF INTERNATIONALLY
RENOWNED FINE ENGLISH EARTHENWARE

HORNSEA'S LARGEST EMPLOYER

5 — Trades, Crafts and Manufacture

As a town with a weekly market dating back to the Middle Ages, Hornsea had long been a centre for craftsmen making wares for sale to folk coming into the town from the surrounding villages. In addition, there were the craftsmen, such as millers and blacksmiths, common to any village, serving the agricultural community. When the railway came the market died out, owing to the competition of Hull's shops and markets, but some of the old established crafts continued. Other crafts, such as those connected with building, flourished as Hornsea grew in size to accommodate the many newcomers taking up residence in the town. Hornsea's position as a centre of artisans and craftsmen is clearly shown by the census return of 1891, the numbers being made up as follows:

Bricklayers, builders, plasterers	12, and 1 apprentice
Stonemasons	1
Plumbers, glaziers and painters	9, and 4 apprentices
Millers	2, and 1 apprentice
Blacksmiths	6, and 1 apprentice
Joiners and wheelwrights	16, and 2 apprentices
Saddlers	1
Cabinet makers	1
Whitesmiths and tinplate workers	3, and 1 apprentice
Boot- and shoemakers	11, and 3 apprentices
Tailors	8, and 3 apprentices
Watchmakers	2
Boat builders	2

The number of men connected with the building industry (everyone from bricklayers to painters in the

Smith's blacksmith's shop on the east side of Market Place. Walter Smith is at the forge in this photograph taken about 1930. The interior had changed little since the end of the 19th century. Walter is operating the hand bellows. His anvil is to the right of the furnace.

Hornsea fishermen at the turn of the century. Left to right: Edward White, Kit Davison, William Bacchus, Smith Usher, Robert Davison, Fred (?), George Naylor and Mike (?). White, Bacchus, Naylor and Robert Davison were operating as fishermen in 1891, Bacchus and Davison being among five lifeboatmen and their families who moved en masse *from Spurn in the Spring of that year. The Davison family originated from Sheringham in Norfolk, from where fishermen came to Hornsea annually, following the herring shoals and also participating in the Hornsea Regatta.*

above table) indicates how Hornsea was still expanding at the end of the 19th century. The town's continuing links with agriculture are shown by the number of blacksmiths, saddlers and millers resident there, not to mention the wheelwrights and joiners, most of whom were still engaged in repairing and making farm equipment. Joiners in Hornsea, however, were probably coming more and more to serve the building industry. There were three blacksmiths' shops in the town, two of them in Market Place and the other in Southgate. Although the bulk of the work there would be in the making and repair of agricultural machines and the shoeing of farm horses, there would also be plenty of shoeing to be done for the horses used by the many delivery men, cab proprietors and other tradesmen in the town. One of the blacksmiths' items of manufacture in the cold winters at the end of the last century was ice-skates.

Footwear was still made locally, as indicated by the number of boot- and shoemakers, although factory-made footwear from such places as Northampton and Leicester had long been available, and in the census James Howlett in Market Place described himself as a boot dealer. In *Bulmer's Directory* of 1892, Burnett's in Newbegin were advertising their 'Family Boot and Shoe Warehouse' where 'a large, choice, and varied assortment of Gentlemen's, Ladies' and Children's Boots and Shoes' were always in stock. However, shoemakers and, particularly, boot-makers continued operating in Hornsea up to the beginning of the Second World War.

The two boat builders in the census were Joseph and William Akester, father and son, who lived in Newbegin. Their clients were probably the dozen or so fishermen who operated from Hornsea, crabbing

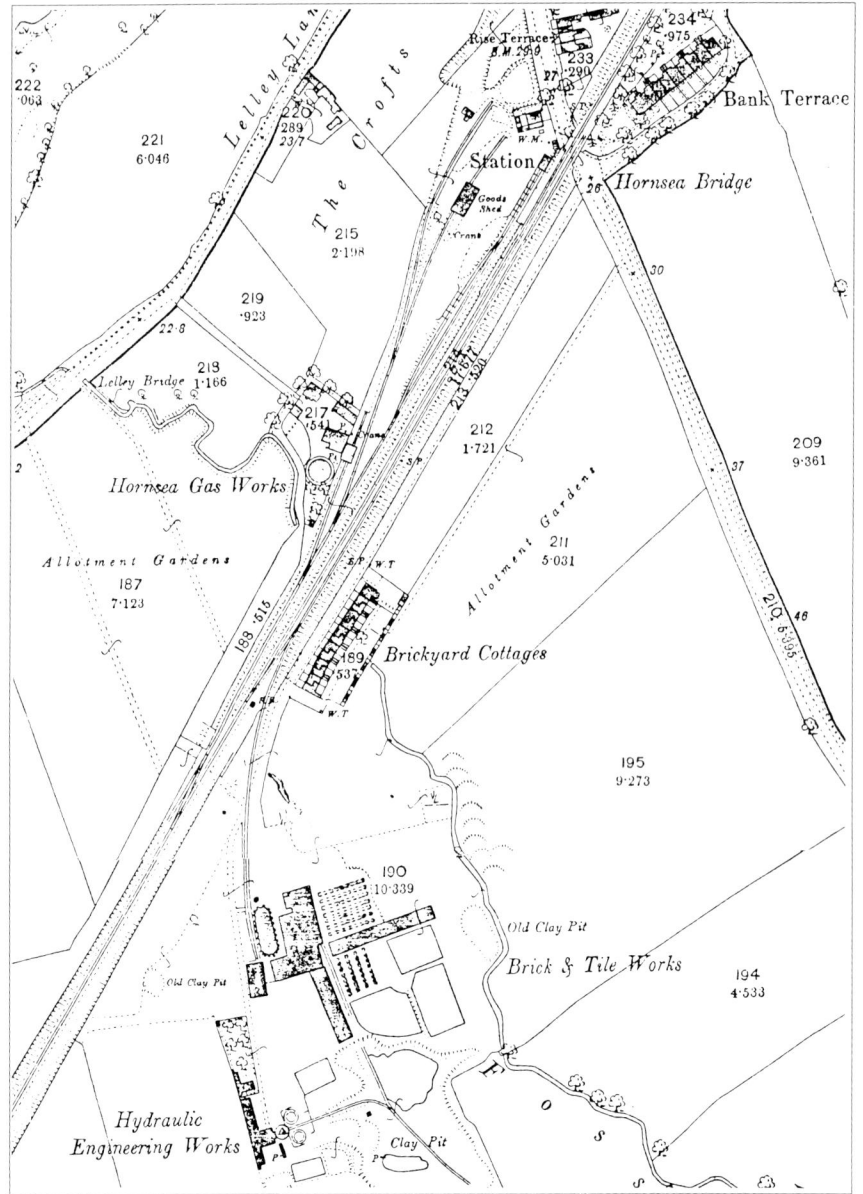

and fishing from cobles. As the town became popular as a holiday resort there was an increase in the demand for fish and shellfish, and a consequent increase in the number of fishermen. It was in the Spring of 1891 that the number of Hornsea's fishermen had been brought up to the dozen by the migration from Spurn of five of the lifeboatmen and their families. The men had sailed their little flotilla of boats from Spurn, laden with crab pots and fishing gear. Their families had been taken up the Humber by sloops to Hull, from where they travelled to Hornsea by train.

One other trade which flourished with the growth of the town, and especially with the increase in wealthy residents, was that of dressmaking. In 1891 there were 31 dressmakers and seamstresses and six apprentices living in Hornsea. Dressmaking

Wade's brickyard. Spur lines, for the delivery of coal, run from the main railway line to both the gas works and the brick works. The clay pit now forms part of the Hornsea Pottery Leisure Park. The lane running from Hornsea Bridge to Brickyard Cottages is now Marlborough Avenue. (Reproduction from the 1891 Ordnance Survey map.)

was, in fact, the largest craft occupation in the town at the time. Whilst the working-class housewife would be making her own clothes, the better-off would be sending for a local dressmaker, if not going to a high-class establishment in Hull.

All these artisans, both men and women, were employed in small one- or two-person enterprises. In addition, however, there were two large manufacturing enterprises, the Hornsea Brick and Tile Works and the Hydraulic Engineering Works, the latter producing pumps for use in all types of industry. Both works were situated together, adjacent to the railway line south of the town, at the end of what is now Marlborough Avenue. The nearby Brickyard Cottages, 13 in number, appear to have housed most of the skilled employees of the Hydraulic Engineering Works. The manager, John Cherry, lived at the Mill House with his wife and three of his children. The two sons were employed at the works, one being a machine fitter and turner and the other an engineering apprentice. Another son, or possibly a younger brother, George Cherry, lived at No. 1 Brickyard Cottages. He was a millwright. Other skilled employees living in the Cottages were another millwright and apprentice millwright, four fitters and an apprentice fitter, one turner, one stationary-engine driver and two blacksmiths. The two blacksmiths are additional to the half dozen already listed and assumed to be working at the forges in Market Place and Southgate. Living in Southgate was another stationary-engine driver, and in Back Southgate was a fitter, both of whom were probably employed at the engineering works.

It is interesting to note that, whereas most of the artisans listed earlier were born locally (i.e. in Hornsea or the East Riding), of those assumed to be employed at the engineering works, few were born locally. The Cherry family were from the East Riding, the two youngest sons being born in Hornsea, but only two other of the works' employees were from the East Riding. The others were born in Berkshire, Norfolk, Gloucestershire, London, North Yorkshire, Kent (two), Cornwall and Lancashire. One of them had been to America as the census return shows one of his sons to have been born there. There must have been a great variety of accents in Brickyard

Brickyard Cottages, Marlborough Avenue. In 1891 the 13 houses were occupied mostly by the skilled workmen of Wade and Cherry's engineering works.

The five-sailed windmill used to drive the puddling mill in Wade's brickyard. The scaffolding is in position for the erection of a chimney for a steam engine which was to supplement wind power.

The site of the mill today.

One of the millstones, now in Hall Garth.

The work force of Wade and Cherry's Hydraulic Engineering Works, with two of the pumps, and employees holding the tools of their trade. The man in the centre with the bowler hat is thought to be Joseph Wade. The man on his right is thought to be John Cherry.

One of the trucks used to transport clay by rail from the pit to the mill. It was excavated from the clay pit in the 1970s. It is now on display in the grounds of the Hornsea Pottery Leisure Park.

Cottages! On the face of it, it looks as though there was some difficulty in recruiting skilled labour locally.

The capital for both the brickyard and the engineering works was supplied by Joseph Armytage Wade, the well-known local entrepreneur and the man who had much to do with the development of Hornsea. His partner in the engineering works was John Cherry, who was the manager of both the engineering works and the brickworks.

Examples of bricks from the Brick and Tile Works occur in many of the houses built in Hornsea between the 1870s and 1890s, and a good example of the Wade interlocking tiles can be seen on the outside walls of the house at the junction of New Road and Westbourne Road. There is a tale that the bricks to build Ventnor House (now Grebe House) at the junction of Back Westgate with Westgate were transported from the brickworks across the Mere one winter when the ice was frozen.

The railway must have been a great asset to the brickworks in bringing coal to fire the kilns and possibly in transporting bricks to other areas, although it may be that the building taking place in Hornsea itself was sufficient to absorb all the output of the works. The railway was also the means of taking coal to the nearby gasworks, another of Joseph Wade's enterprises. The area of the brickyard was dominated by a five-sail windmill driving two huge mill-stones running on edge, 'puddling' the clay to a fine state for moulding. Also helping to dominate the sky-line was the 75-foot-high chimney of the kiln. The clay was excavated from a clay pit on the site and hauled up to the mill in trucks on rails.

Joseph Wade died in 1896 and, although the master of the Hornsea's Mixed School ascribed the fall in attendance the following year to the fact that many children had left the district owing to the closure of the brickyard, it would seem, in fact, that it was the engineering works that closed. In 1897 John Cherry was described as the manager of the brickworks only. By 1901 he was no longer living in the town, and the Hornsea Brick and Tile Company Ltd., operating on the same site, had come into existence. It seems to have closed at some time between 1913 and 1921. Today, a large part of the former site is occupied by Hornsea Pottery. The old clay pit still exists as the picturesque, tree-flanked wildfowl lake in the Pottery leisure park. The bed of the rail-track which ran from the main line to the works can still be seen. One of the millstones from the puddling mill lies in Hall Garth, near to the entrance from Cinema Street. Brickyard Cottages form part of the terraces of houses in Marlborough Avenue. Mill House, John Cherry's former residence, still stands, and the offices of the brickworks are now used by the pottery. However, the raw material for their product comes not from the soils of Hornsea but from distant Cornwall and Devon.

The pottery continues the tradition of manufacturing in Hornsea. However, except for the building trades, few, if any, of the old crafts survive, although they died hard. In 1937 Hornsea still had two watchmakers, a blacksmith and a tailor's shop; William Arksey and Harry Robinson were still making boots, as their fathers had been in 1891; the Walker family, tinplate workers in 1891, were continuing in business. But these seem to be the last of Hornsea's craftsmen making goods for sale in their own shops. The modern trend was illustrated by the fact that Frederick Simpson, who had been apprenticed to William Arksey's father as a shoemaker in 1891, was only advertising as a repairer of boots and shoes in 1937.

With its brickworks and engineering works, its men still plying the old crafts, and the new developments bringing in more men from the

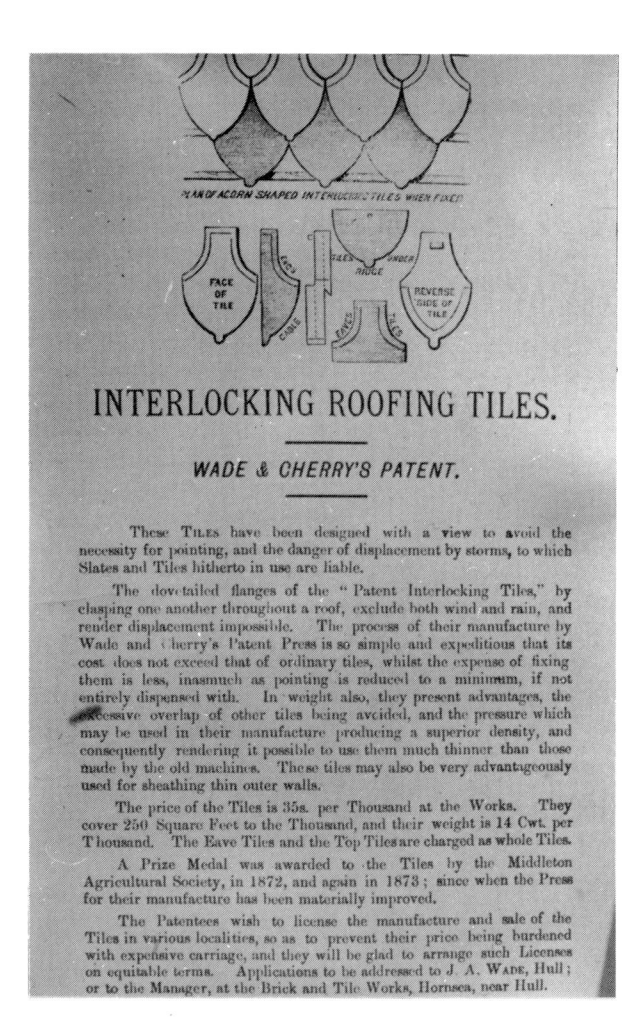

Wade and Cherry's patent interlocking tiles. The last paragraph indicates that, despite the railway, the cost of transport could greatly increase the price of heavy materials. It confirms the view that the railway line was used more to bring coal to fire the brick kilns than to export bricks from the yard. There was probably a sufficient demand from the builders of Hornsea to absorb the output of Wade's works.

building trades, Hornsea probably had its highest ever proportion of trades- and craftsmen in its population in the last quarter of the 19th century.

House at the corner of New Road and Westbourne Road clad in Wade and Cherry's patent acorn-shaped tiles. In 1891 the house was occupied by Alfred Maw of the Hull firm of Maw, Till and Kirke, furniture makers.

PERFECT MATCH

SOMETHING OLD
SOMETHING NEW
ANY OUTFIT MADE
SPECIALLY FOR YOU

. . . the complete package

Original ideas for the perfect wedding

Market Place, Hornsea. Tel: (0964) 532334
or evening appointments by arrangement

6 — Farmers and Farmworkers

In Hornsea parish in 1891 there were about 30 farmers of all kinds, ranging from the cowkeepers, working on their own, to the large farmers, who might employ many men, especially at harvest time. Providing the all-year-round labour were the 50 or so agricultural workers living in the parish. Compared with today the numbers are high, but the old-timers of the '90s could look back a generation and remember the times when there was double that number of farm workers in a total population only half of what it was in 1891.

In the 1890s Hornsea still depended very much on its farmers for a great part of its economy, not only because of the produce and the jobs they provided but also because of the various trades in the village, such as corn-milling, smithying and wheel-making, which they sustained.

The outlying farmsteads, like those at Southorpe and Northorpe, were of the usual pattern: a foldyard surrounded by the house on the west, a high barn and granary on the north giving shelter from cold winds, and cowhouses and stables on the east. In or near the town itself, which was where most of the dairy farmers had their premises, farm buildings were more confined. These various farms required a total labour force of 70 or 80, counting the farmers themselves, with extra labour being brought in at busy times of the year.

One vital part of the work force which did not appear in the census were the horses on the farm. They varied from the very heavy hairy-legged shires, which took a lot of grooming when working on land that was wet and muddy, to the cleaner-legged Clydesdales. On a farm of around 200 acres there would be from eight to ten working horses, with perhaps one or two mares kept for breeding as well as young horses being prepared to work on the farm or to be sold into the towns for carting work.

When the teams were working together, or going to and from the fields, the wagoner (second in seniority to the foreman) always went first with his pair of horses, followed by the third lad, then the

Southorpe Farm from the west. A typical arrangement of a farmhouse with the farm buildings on the north side. One of the few remaining working farms within the bounds of Hornsea parish.

fourth lad, right down to the least lad with his pair last. Woe betide the lad who got out of his proper order; he was soon told to get back into line. Because of the bad state of the roads, four horses were needed to pull a loaded wagon, which was then usually the responsibility of the wagoner.

In addition to the farm horses, most farmers kept a trap horse or pony that could trot to the station with the milk float, and take the butter and eggs to the market or the family to church on Sunday.

The permanent farm workers often lived-in on the farm, and in the census are usually described as farm servants. They lodged in the farmhouse, unless there was a foreman's, or hind's, house on the farm, in which case the hind's wife would be paid to lodge and feed them. Depending on the size of the farm, two, three, four or even more men and lads, and perhaps a girl to do the housework and some of the lighter jobs around the farm, would be hired for the year at the Martinmas hirings. From Brockholme, on the Seaton Road, 60-year-old Frederick Feaster farmed 300 acres with the help of his son and five farm servants ranging in age from 15 to 31. The household also included Laura Robson, an 18-year-old maid, to help Mrs. Feaster about the house. The hirings were held in the towns and some of the larger villages in November time. Hornsea was a centre for such hirings, which there took place on the last Monday in November. The men would gather in Market Place and meet with the different farmers to bargain for a year's work. The wage, when it was agreed, was paid at the end of the year, just before the next hirings. Occasionally, the farmer might make a small advance of wages if there was a desperate need on the part of the employee. When the agreement on wage was reached at the hirings, the farmer would give his new

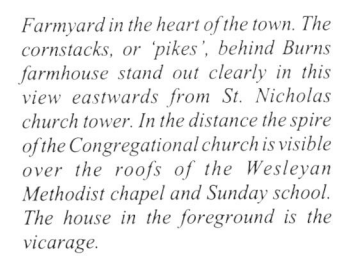

Farmyard in the heart of the town. The cornstacks, or 'pikes', behind Burns farmhouse stand out clearly in this view eastwards from St. Nicholas church tower. In the distance the spire of the Congregational church is visible over the roofs of the Wesleyan Methodist chapel and Sunday school. The house in the foreground is the vicarage.

Horses and farmworkers at Weather Hill Farm. The farm was just outside the Hornsea boundary but the track to it led from Lelley Lane, and Weather Hill Lodge, where a shepherd lived in 1891, was within the bounds of Hornsea.

servant a shilling (5p) or half a crown (12½p), called a 'fest', which, if accepted, meant the agreement was binding. Girls seeking employment at the Hornsea hirings, rather than having to stand around in Market Place or in one of the public houses, were allowed to wait in the Parish Room after its completion in 1887. They were often interviewed by the farmers' wives before being offered a position.

In the 1890s, a lad of 14 or 15 years of age might start off on a wage of £8 a year which, after a few years' experience, would rise to £18. Girls' and women's wages were similar. Farm foremen earned about £25 and usually received a higher fest at the hiring. All food and accommodation throughout the year were provided by the farmer, and one consideration that might might sway a worker in the acceptance of a job could often be the reputation of the farmer's, or his hind's, wife for her cooking!

The next nearest towns where hirings took place were Bridlington, Driffield, Beverley, Hedon and Hull. Hirings also took place at the villages of Beeford and Aldbrough. When the hiring system was at its height the large towns could easily draw several thousand farm servants in search of a new position. At Hornsea, however, at the end of the century, when the system was on the wane, the numbers were usually below a hundred. Even then, workers could be drawn from quite a wide area, and the places of birth of farm workers in the Hornsea census show that they originated from all parts of the Holderness area as well as from places further afield such as Lincolnshire and Norfolk. The birth-places of Frederick Feaster's five hands in 1891 were Aldbrough, Withernsea, Beverley, Hull and Ireland.

The week of the hirings was a holiday for farm workers and it could be a very riotous time when, as at Hornsea, 50 lads and perhaps 30 girls met up after living on out-of-the-way farms for a year. They had a year's wages to spend, and stallholders, showmen and cheap jacks moved into the town to help relieve them of their hard-earned money. Hirings week was often a subject for complaint by Isaac Gilman, the master of the National School, either because of truancy by his pupils joining their elder brethren in the holidaying or because of the noise made by bands of farm lads on the Green outside his school.

Some farm workers were employed by the day. In the census they are referred to as agricultural labourers rather than farm servants. They might live with their families in cottages near the farm or in the town itself. Some single farm workers were living in lodgings. Working on a farm in the 1890s meant long hours, from six in the morning till six at night, six days a week. Unless the weather was very bad there was no excuse to go for shelter. The work could be very heavy, forking sheaves or manure, or carrying 16-stone sacks of barley or 18-stone sacks of wheat from the threshing machine and up a ladder into the granary. Accidents were frequent, and many farm workers walked lame, or were to be seen with stooped backs in old age.

Agricultural wages were poor, although not as poor as they might have been had there been no competition for labour offered by the industries and building projects in Hull and even in Hornsea itself. In the 1870s, Hornsea farmers had grumbled when the Hornsea Steam Brick and Tile Works had offered wages of £30-£40 a year, thus pushing up the wages in the locality. By the 1890s the wage of a day labourer on a farm was in the region of 15 to 16 shillings (75-80p) a week, but always with the risk of being stood off if the weather was too bad to work. As a general labourer on a building site in Hull a man could earn 25 shillings (£1.25) for a week's work, which included Saturday afternoon off.

When extra workmen were needed on the farms during busy times they might be recruited from the bands of Irishmen who came over from their native country during harvest time. They followed the ripening harvest from south to north, usually reaching the Dales before returning southwards for the potato harvests. Another source of extra labour was the schoolboys. The school holiday was fixed to coincide with the harvest, but the school log contains many instances of boys being kept from school if the harvest was late, as was often recorded in the last quarter of the 19th century, when cold, wet conditions prevailed. It was illegal to employ children during school hours, and the master of the school could report the matter to the Attendance Officer or, ultimately, to the magistrates. Usually, it was enough to point the matter out to the erring employer, as on the occasion in August 1892 when Isaac Gilman found it necessary to write to Joseph Wade's foreman about three boys working on his farm. The boys were back at school the following Monday. As Joseph Wade was the chairman of the school managers, it would not have looked well if his foreman had been brought before the magistrates for employing school children!

In the 1890s the ever-energetic Joseph Wade was one of the leading farmers in Hornsea. As described elsewhere in these pages, he was concerned in many other enterprises, and had probably turned to farming as a hobby. He had a farm of 350 acres with reputedly the best sheep, horses and farm machinery in the district. When his stock was sold off after his death in 1896, the field where the auction took place was described as having the 'appearance of an agricultural show of implements'. No doubt, Wade had many times exhibited at the Hornsea Agricultural Show, held in alternate years in Hornsea. The show took place in July or August and in 1891 was a day for an official holiday for the Hornsea school children.

The last quarter of the 19th century was a time of poor returns for British farmers. To the problems of cold, wet summers were added serious outbreaks of animal and crop disease. Worst of all, for the farmer, were the increasing imports of cheaper foodstuffs from abroad. By the 1890s, besides the cheap wheat coming from the United States, there was cheap beef from South America, lamb and butter from New

Zealand, and bacon and butter from Denmark. Many small farmers went out of business. Others took on other work such as carting bricks, or coal, or gravel for road mending — anything to try and make a living. Others converted more of their land to pasture for cows — one thing that could not be imported from abroad was fresh milk — and Hornsea's high population and holiday trade probably encouraged more dairy farming than in the neighbouring villages.

Hornsea farmers were perhaps lucky in that they had easy access to distant markets via the railway, but they would still try to sell their produce locally and, likewise, purchase as many of their needs in the town as they could in order to avoid transport costs. There would be frequent visits to the three blacksmiths in the town for horses to be shod or implements to be mended, to Henry Carr, saddler and harness maker in Market Place, to Thomas Foley, wheelwright and joiner, on Mereside, and to the Peers, father and son, slaughtermen in Southgate and Back Southgate. During the late autumn and winter, as the threshing machines got busy in the stackyards, there would be carts trundling with sacks of corn up to the windmill in Atwick Road or to the railway station for despatch to the more modern mills in Hull. Some of the dairy farmers, or cowkeepers as they were listed in the census, had their buildings in the town — John Harker at White House in Southgate, John Witty in Back Southgate, Robert Barker in Westgate, and Elizabeth Burn at Burn's Farm (now the Museum) in Newbegin — and twice a day for most of the year they would need to drive their cows back to the dairies for milking from their pastures on the Bewholme, Atwick and Seaton Roads. From these farms there would also be the daily journeys of the milk-floats, not to mention the less frequent, but more noticeable, removal of manure. In the 1890s the townspeople were certainly very much aware of the farmers in the Hornsea community!

However, Hornsea's farming population was dwindling owing not only to the recession in agriculture but also to the increased use of machinery. Increased efficiency in agricultural production has continued apace and today, although the acreage of land under cultivation in the parish of Hornsea is not much different from what it was 100 years ago, it can be dealt with by far fewer men using modern machines. The machines are sold and repaired by central dealers, the produce goes off the farm in large lorries, and farming has very little impact on modern Hornsea. Of the 30 or so premises that were farms in Hornsea in 1891, only five are working farms today.

EASTGATE TRAVEL

ABTA A9843

Proprietor; Ron Hughes, P.Q.R.C.

Leisure and Business Travel

**Air and Coach Tickets
Group Travel Arrangements**

*Contact the team for information
and a quotation*

**BANK HOUSE, BANK STREET
HORNSEA, HU18 1AE
Tel: (0964) 532679
Fax: (0964) 536192**

J.R.Higson
& Partners
OPTOMETRISTS OPTICIANS

BEVERLEY
36 Market Place.
0482 861052

HORNSEA
104 Newbegin.
0964 532589

SCARBOROUGH
40 Falsgrave Road.
0723 361433

DRIFFIELD
100 Middle Street South.
0377 253039

HULL
239 Beverley Road
0482 493125

WITHERNSEA
120 Queen Street.
0964 612012

323 Holderness Road.
0482 23583

Ground Floor Rooms
Home Visits
Ladies & Gentlemens
fashion frames from £18.99
Designer Frames
Contact Lenses & Solutions

HEDON
18 Souttergate.
0482 896803

44 Savile Street.
0482 29122

B. A. WHITTLE
CHEMISTS

Come and see the widest range:

* From leading names in toiletries for both ladies and men
* Suntan preparations and sunglasses
* Wine-making, Home Brewing
* Gifts for babies and toddlers
* Films, cameras and accessories
* Health foods and diabetic foods

130-132 Newbegin, Hornsea. Tel: (0964) 533242

B. A. WHITTLE
CHEMISTS

* We provide full NHS dispensing service
* For colostomy, ileostomy and urostomy
* Oxygen supply
* Hosiery and trusses
* As well as homeopathic, allopathic medicine

FREE HOME DELIVERIES of repeat prescriptions willingly made. Simply ask

OPEN MONDAY TO FRIDAY 8.45 AM - 6.00 PM
SATURDAY 8.45 AM - 5.00 PM

130-132 Newbegin, Hornsea. Tel: (0964) 533242

7 — Church and Chapel

There were four branches of the Christian religion flourishing in Hornsea 100 years ago: the Church of England, the Wesleyan Methodist, the Primitive Methodist, and the Congregationalist. Each had its own place of worship and, since the coming of the railway in 1864, each had spent considerable sums of money on their church buildings. The Primitive Methodists had in fact anticipated the increase in congregations which the railway would bring when they had planned the building of a new chapel in 1862, the year the Hull and Hornsea Railway Company was formed. However, the site for the building was not obtained until 1864, and the new chapel was opened in Market Place in July the following year. A writer to the *Primitive Methodist Magazine* in November 1865 commented, 'They had the strongest reason to believe that, as Railway communication was now opened to the place, its population would soon greatly increase. Hence, believing in the good Providence of God that the time had come for them to considerably enlarge their borders, they have erected Chapel, School Room and Vestries'. Their confidence was not misplaced: between 1861 and 1871 Hornsea's population went up from 1,063 to 1,685, and attendance at all four churches increased accordingly.

The Primitives' new chapel cost them £1,250. In 1870 the Wesleyans built a new chapel in Newbegin

The former Primitive Methodist chapel in Market place, built in 1865 at a cost of £1,250.

The Wesleyan Methodist chapel in Newbegin completed in 1870 at a cost of about £4,500.

and five years later added a Sunday school. The total outlay was £4,500. The Congregational church at the corner of New Road and Cliff Road was opened in 1874 and cost about £3,000. Meanwhile, in 1867-8, £3,500 had been spent by the Anglicans on the restoration of the old parish church of St. Nicholas. In 1887 £200 was spent on the building of the parish room close by the church.

The church of St. Nicholas had been in existence since before the Norman Conquest. No doubt religious fervour varied over the centuries. Certainly, in the 18th century it was at a low ebb. There was no resident vicar and the influence of the Anglican Church was declining. When a group of Methodists arrived in the village around 1770 they found the spiritual condition of the population, consisting mainly of fishermen and agricultural workers, to be deplorable. The group began meeting in a room at Low Hall (now the White House) in Southgate but, eventually, in 1814 bought a plot of land 15 yards by 12 in Back Southgate for the erection of their own chapel. When completed, the building could seat 250 worshippers. When the new chapel was built in Newbegin half a century later, the old one was sold to a Hull butcher for £200. He in turn sold it to General William Booth of the Salvation Army for £210 in 1885. In 1890, a group consisting of Joseph Armytage Wade, Thomas Gregson, seed crusher, and John Bull Ridges, schoolmaster, all of Hornsea, and Thomas Bainton, farmer, of Arram Hall, purchased the building for £150. It then became the headquarters of the Hornsea and District Liberal Club. In 1908 it became yet again a place of worship when Benjamin Haworth-Booth of Rowlston Hall registered it as the First Church of Christ Scientist. The building appears to have been converted for use as a warehouse at some later date.

The Primitive Methodists came into existence, initially in the Midlands, as a breakaway group from the Wesleyans, in 1812. The first Primitive Methodist chapel in Hornsea was built in Westgate in 1835. It could seat about 150 persons. After the building of the new chapel in Market Place the old chapel was pulled down to make way for the minister's manse.

The Congregationalists, or Independents as they were first known, were one of the earliest dissenting groups, with their beginnings in the 17th century. They appear to have become first established in Hornsea in 1798 following a visit by Rev. George Lambert of the Fish Street Congregational Church in Hull. The first chapel in Hornsea was built in Southgate in 1808. On the day of the opening, George Lambert arose at 4 a.m. and walked from Hull in order

The Congregational church, a familiar landmark in Hornsea, built in 1874 at a cost of £3,000. The manse is to the left of the church. Note the condition of the roads.

Saint Nicholas parish church and the parish room. Between 1867 and 1868, £3,500 was spent on restoring the church. The parish room was built in 1887 at a cost of £200.

> PLACES OF WORSHIP.
> *Parish Church* (St. Nicholas)—Rev. E. L. H. Tew, M.A., vicar; 10-30 a.m. and 6-30 p.m. Holy Communion on first and third Sunday in each month, after Morning Prayers; other Sundays at 8 a.m. Litany, Holy Baptism, and Catechism on the first Sunday in the month at 3 p.m.; Litany on third Sunday at 4 p.m. Holy days—Communion at 8 a.m., Morning Prayer at 11 a.m. Wednesday and Friday—Litany at 12-5p.m. Daily—Morning Prayer, at 8 a.m.; Evening Prayer, 5-30 p.m. in winter, 4-30 p.m. in Summer. Saints' Days—7-30 p.m.
> *Congregational*—10-30 a.m., 6-30 p.m.; Thursday, 7-30 p.m.
> *Primitive Methodist*—Revs. F. G. Wallis and J. W. Everingham; 10-30 a.m. and 6-30 p.m.; Thursday, 7-30 p.m.; Monday, Prayer Meeting, at 7-30 p.m.; Saturday, Band Meeting, at 7-30 p.m.
> *Wesleyan*—Revs. W. G. Hall and R. Garbett; 10-30 a.m. and 6-30 p.m.; Wednesday, 7-30 p.m.; Friday, Prayer Meeting, 7-30 p.m.

Bulmer's Directory, *1892, showing the number of services held during the week at the different places of worship.*

to preach at the first morning service in the new chapel. The building, which could seat between 300 and 350, still stands at the corner of King Street.

There are no direct figures by which a comparison can be made of the size of the congregations at the four churches in the 1890s. Saint Nicholas Church had seating accommodation for 760 persons, and the chapels of the Wesleyans and the Congregationalists had sittings for 485 and 470, respectively, with extra accommodation for Sunday School children. No figure is available for the seating at the Primitive chapel. In 1902, however, it was found necessary to provide additional seating and in the 1920s, the building was accommodating average attendances of 300. In the 1890s all four churches had morning and evening services on Sundays, as well as weekday meetings or services. At the only religious census taken in Britain, on 30 March 1851, there had been 100 present at matins at St. Nicholas, and over 100 at each of the evening services of the other three churches. These figures did not include Sunday School children. At that time Hornsea's population was 945, less than half of what it was in 1891.

At St. Nicholas the total money taken in collections between Easter 1891 and Easter 1892 was £171. This was at a time when coppers in the collection were common, and a shilling (5p) was considered a princely offering. In the same period £182 was collected at the Wesleyan chapel, including money taken at occasional mid-week lectures. Membership at that time was approaching 140, although actual attendance figures tended to be well in excess of membership. The receipts from the quarterages and weekly offerings of the Primitives, which drew their support more from working-class people, was almost £66 in 1891. In that year the maximum membership was 121 although, as for the Wesleyans, attendance figures tended to be in excess of membership (for example, in 1864, when the Primitives' membership was 50, the average attendance of worshippers was about 120). There are no comparable figures for the Congregational church, but the fact that they had found it necessary, like the Methodists, to move to larger premises from a building which, in their case, was capable of seating 350, suggests that they were prepared for some large congregations. In all, it might be said with confidence, that in the 1890s each of the four churches in Hornsea could expect attendances of at least 200, and far more on special occasions or in the holiday season (in 1891 the highest monthly collections at both the Wesleyan chapel and St. Nicholas were in the August, and the highest quarterly collection at the Primitive chapel was in the quarter ending September).

At St. Nicholas the conduct of the services was entirely in the hands of the vicar, Rev. Edmund

Lawrence Hemstead Tew, although laymen read the lessons on occasions. Four churchwardens and four sidesmen were elected at the Vestry meeting each year. Both the Hornsea Wesleyan and the Hornsea Primitive churches were the heads of circuits covering many of the villages around. In the 1890s the Wesleyan circuit consisted of 19 churches extending from Garton in the south to Atwick in the north and westward to Leven. In 1891 the ministers were Rev. Walter Hall and Rev. Frederick Church, who both lived in Hornsea. They were assisted by 23 lay preachers, 12 of whom lived in Hornsea, and seven trialists, five of whom came from Hornsea. A note on the circuit 'plans' for that period drew the attention of trialist lay preachers to the fact that 'No preacher can become a fully accredited local preacher until he has read the fifty three Standard Sermons of Mr. Wesley and his notes on the New Testament'. With 19 churches to supply each Sunday for two services even 23 preachers required help and this came from Hull. These men were well catered for as to travelling arrangements, as the advice printed on the plan shows:

'The Hull conveyance (when trains will not serve) will leave Mr. Annison's stable at Witham at 8.30 a.m. prompt for the Aldbrough journey and 12 o'clock for afternoon and evening when there is no morning service.

'The Skirlaugh preacher comes from Hull by the morning train and meets the conveyance on Burton Constable bridge after evening service.

'Special notice. The trains from and to Hull will serve from May 1st and all through the summer and enable the Brethren to return home after evening services and so save the cost of conveyance.'

The Primitive Methodist circuit contained 13 churches extending from Aldbrough to Atwick and west to Leven. The ministers in 1891 were Rev. Stephen Oates and Rev. Joseph Everingham, both resident in Hornsea. They were assisted by 24 lay preachers, eight of whom came from Hornsea. Of the eight trialists on the 1892 plan, five came from Hornsea. One well-known local Primitive lay preacher was Rose Carr, the woman who ran a carrier's business from Eastgate. Better known amongst the members of his Church, perhaps, was William Robinson, a shoemaker in Southgate, who, at the age of 94 in 1940, was still to be found on occasions occupying his seat in the choir. He became a member at the Market Place chapel in 1865 and a local preacher in 1866. In his early days it was not unusual for him to take as many as 28 appointments in a quarter which, in the days before the bicycle, could mean walking anything up to 20 miles on a Sunday and as many as 150 miles in a quarter. He was born in Hull in 1846 and had the rare distinction among the members in 1940 of having been baptized by William Clowes, co-founder, with Hugh Bourne, of the Primitive Methodist movement. In 1938 a letter of congratulation for all his work was sent to Robinson from the annual conference, held that year in Hull. The preachers' plan for the 1892 September quarter contained an advertisement for *The Primitive Methodist* and *The Primitive Methodist World* which 'are devoted to the spread of Connexional intelligence and matters of special interest to our people. May be obtained direct from the publishers post free for 1s 9d per quarter, or from any newsagent for One Penny Weekly. Mr. W. Robinson (Hornsea) is agent for the latter'.

On census day, 1891, the Congregationalist manse was unoccupied but only, it seems, because the minister, Rev. David Tysil Evans, a 38-year-old bachelor, preferred to live in lodgings at 8 Wilton Terrace rather than go to the expense of furnishing a large house. The Congregationalists had considerable influence in the town and many of the leading members of the community were members. Each congregation was quite independent of all others, having its own pastor, deciding its own doctrine and acknowledging no higher earthly religious authority.

All four denominations ran Sunday Schools, the three dissenting groups having purpose-built accommodation as part of their church buildings. At the Primitives' chapel the school room was under the main hall, which was approached up a broad flight of steps. In 1895 it was realised that the school room was too small for the numbers attending and it was decided to build a new one, which was opened as an extension to the rear of the chapel in 1897.

Saint Nicholas held its Sunday School in the day school, which was itself an Anglican establishment, down at the Mere side. We know of only one Sunday School teacher at the Anglican Sunday School. That was the Vicar's wife, Jane Tew, who once had cause to complain about the bad behaviour of the scholars, which she attributed to the poor discipline at the day school. Both the Mixed School at the Mere-side and the Infants' School in Westgate were Church of England schools and, for most Hornsea parents of limited means, were the only schools to which they could send their children, whatever their own denomination. At the Mixed School the vicar took Scripture classes every day of the week (the children having to sing his favourite hymn, *Fair waved the golden corn,* as he entered the school door), and his wife and the Misses Tew frequently visited the Infant School. The Mixed School was examined in religious knowledge once a year by the Diocesan Inspector. Some typical entries in the school log book, by the master, Isaac Gilman, are as follows:

'July 20th 1891. Diocesan Examination. Conducted as usual by the Revd. E. J. Barry, the Assistant Diocesan Inspector. Time — 10 to 12.45. Vicar questioned Divn. II on the Catechism and the Master the Upper Divn.

'Aug. 6th 1891. Diocesan Inspector's report — "Tested for knowledge on Old and New Testaments, Catechism and Prayer Book and for repetition of Scripture, Hymns, Collects and Catechism. The ratings ranged from 'Good' to 'Excellent'. In the two upper divisions a very useful explanation of the catechism has been successfully given. The character of the answering on the Biblical work continues to improve."

'Oct. 30th 1891. The Scripture lessons have been well appreciated during the last few weeks. Finished Genesis this morning. Vicar only present once this week as he has been at the Diocesan Conference at York.'

Whether all this religious instruction roused any enthusiasm for church-going is debatable, as the following entry in the log suggests:

'May 8th 1891. Closed yesterday, being Holy Thursday. Had told all the children to be here at 10 & to go with the teachers to church at 10.30 but only about 20 came.' (The average attendance at the school in 1891 was 165.)

Perhaps it was because the Established Church in Hornsea had the minds of the children during the week that the Dissenting groups laid particular emphasis on Sunday School work. In 1896 the Wesleyans had 120 Sunday scholars taught by 29 teachers (a pupil-teacher ratio that Isaac Gilman and his two assistants at the day school must have sorely envied!). The Primitives had 42 scholars and 16 teachers in 1864, and in 1924 no fewer than 173 scholars taught by 38 teachers.

The Congregationalists were particularly active among the young, according to Charles Booth, the great social reformer, with such activities as camera and tennis clubs. Booth, commenting at the beginning of this century, also remarked that the Congregational Church was 'not one for the poor', but was very strong among middle-class people. 'They were more social than religious.' They had great choirs and were also politically active. These last two statements appear to be true of the Hornsea group. It had a choir which, in January 1891, was presenting the *Messiah,* with the assistance of local friends (including members of the Wesleyans' choir) 'and a powerful contingent of the Hull Harmonic Society'. A hint of the political associations is given by the fact that the manse in Cliff Road was built at the expense of John Bainton, of Arram Hall, whose son, Thomas, helped purchase the old Wesleyan chapel in Back Southgate for use as the headquarters of the Liberal Club.

Of the three great Nonconformist churches, Booth considered that the Wesleyans were more joyous in their mode of life than either the Congregationalists or the Baptists (who had no church in Hornsea) and their services made great use of music, having in many instances a full choir, organ and sometimes even an orchestra. They had the rich heritage of the hymns of Charles and John Wesley. 'God is a God of gladness', said a Wesleyan monthly magazine. The church in Newbegin had a fine pipe organ and a large choir which took a very active part, not only in the worship, but also in the general life of the church. The principal singer in the performance of the *Messiah* already referred to was Miss Ethel Holmes, a member of the Wesleyan choir and daughter of Thomas Barton Holmes, head of the Hull firm of tanners and a prominent Wesleyan. On the same occasion the band was led by T. B. Holmes, junior. Thomas Holmes, senior, himself played the organ for the services in the chapel.

Like the Congregationalists, the Wesleyan Church was associated with the middle class of society, although there is ample evidence that many members of the working class were to be found in its membership. The Primitives, however, were much more closely associated with the working class. Strong indications of these class differences are apparent from what we know of some of the leading members of the four churches in Hornsea. Of the dozen laymen prominent in the affairs of St. Nicholas — churchwardens, sidesmen, honorary auditors and others mentioned at the annual meetings — the majority lived in fair-sized houses in the newer residential area at the east end of Newbegin or in the New Road region. Only shopkeepers living next to their business premises, such as John Heslop, chemist and churchwarden, resided in the old part of the town. Another indication of the position of these men in at least the middle stratum of society was their employment of domestic servants. On census day 1891 seven of the dozen had one or two servants living-in. The Reverend Edmund Tew, himself, had two servants as did Rev. Walter Hall, the Wesleyan minister, living in Grosvenor Terrace in New Road. The other Wesleyan minister, Rev. Frederick Church, lived at Cliff Villas in Cliff Road and had one servant. Although the Congregational manse was unoccupied on census day, its size (it still stands as The Old Manse House in Cliff Road) indicates the class of person it was intended for. The one member of the Congregationalists, besides the minister, whom we know of was William Gibson, the Hull paint and varnish manufacturer, who lived at The Leylands on Atwick Road and had two servants. The Wesleyans were similarly generally well off. Thomas Holmes lived at Elim Lodge and employed five domestic servants. Of the eight local men mentioned in the Hornsea Wesleyan collection journal for the 1890s, four had shops or workshops in Newbegin or Market Place. The others lived in the fashionable areas on the outskirts of the town. All, except David Smith, the blacksmith in Market Place, Cook Laking, the draper in Newbegin, and George Dunn, a gardener living in Headlands View, had from one to three servants in the household.

It may be significant that when the Congregationalists and Wesleyans moved to new sites in the 1870s they chose positions in the better class area for their churches, although it could have been the availability of building sites that governed their choice. The Primitives stayed close to their working-class flock when they built their new chapel in Market Place. Very few of their leading personalities kept servants or lived in large houses. The Reverend Stephen Oates lived at the manse on the site of the old chapel in Westgate and kept one servant. In 1891 the other minister, Joseph

Everingham, was lodging with one of the lay preachers, John Witty, a cowkeeper in Back Southgate. Varied indeed were the occupations of the lay preachers and officers of the Hornsea Primitives, with a saddler, postman, tailor, corn miller, gardener, farm foreman, general labourer, shoemaker, fisherman, bricklayer, railway porter and platelayer amongst their ranks. Of the 20 laymen recorded in connection with the Primitive chapel, 14 lived in the old area of the town: in Market Place, at the west end of Newbegin or between Southgate and Mereside. Only James Holmes, a farmer living on Bewholme Road, and William Parker, a grocer in Market Place, had a domestic servant in the household. Seven of the members lived in houses of only three or four rooms. It was with pride that the Hornsea centenary programme in 1965 referred to the Primitive movement as 'this Working Class Church'.

Despite the differences in class and religious outlook within the four denominations, there seems to have been a remarkable spirit of harmony, which was not always evident elsewhere between Church and Chapel. It has already been mentioned that the Wesleyans joined the Congregational church in their 1891 production of the *Messiah*. When the Primitive Methodist chapel was re-opened in 1875 following renovation and the installation of a new stove and harmonium, the celebratory tea was provided by the ladies of St. Nicholas Church and of the Wesleyan Methodists. In February 1903 the Primitive Methodist Trustees decided that Mr. T. B. Holmes (a Wesleyan, as already noted) be asked to take the chair at the following meeting, should Mr. J. Rank not be able to do so. In 1869 Joseph Armytage Wade, nominally an Anglican, contributed a donation of £20 towards the building of the new Wesleyan chapel. Wade also assisted the Congregationalists by reducing the price of the site for the New Road chapel from £390 to £290. Wade was churchwarden of St. Nicholas from 1879 to 1882, although he did decline re-election in 1883 'because he wished to be at liberty to attend whatever place of worship he chose.' Whether this meant there were differences between Wade and the Anglican Church we do not know. If there were, they did not prevent Wade continuing as

Joseph Wade's gravestone in St. Nicholas churchyard. The Wades had a family vault and so the interment (in 1896) was permitted even though the churchyard had been closed to burials since the opening of the cemetery in Eastgate. It is said that as the head of Wade's funeral procession was entering the church the end was just leaving Bridge railway station.

one of the feoffees of the Church lands in Hornsea up to the time of his death in 1896, or his daughter being married in St. Nicholas church in 1885, or his own eventual interment in the churchyard.

The ecumenical spirit continues in Hornsea today, particularly with the group known as 'North Holderness Churches Together'. The group, with members from the Anglicans, the Methodists, the United Reformed Church (formerly the Congregationalists), the Roman Catholics and the Pentecostals, holds services in the different churches, with ministers from the different denominations preaching. It could be regarded as the continuation of a trend which began over 100 years ago in Hornsea. Nationally, the Wesleyans and the Primitives merged in the 1930s and Hornsea's Primitive Methodist chapel is now closed as a place of worship. It has served in recent years as a snooker hall, night club and housing accommodation. At the time of writing (1993) it is closed but there are plans for it to be used by the Pentecostal Church, once more as a place of worship.

The Copper Kettle

Licensed Restaurant

Meals served all day - every day

Private functions our speciality

Proprietors:
Tony and Gillian Cousins
who will be pleased to serve you
at

The Market Place Hornsea

Telephone: (0964) 532563

8 — The Schools

The census of 1891 shows there to have been 27 people engaged in teaching in Hornsea. Only five of them were men. The list includes seven governesses, of whom two were living-in with families.

Hornsea was well provided with educational establishments if we are to compare it with other sizable East Yorkshire villages of the same period. According to *Bulmer's Directory* of 1892 there were in Hornsea a total of nine academies and schools, including the 'Mixed' School by the Mere-side and the Infants' School in Westgate, serving a population of 2,013. The same directory shows Flamborough, with a population of 1,288, Holme-on-Spalding-Moor, with a population of 1,815, and Cottingham, with a population of 3,800, to each have only one school.

There were two dame schools in Hornsea in 1892. One was run by Sarah Bellerby, a 51-year-old widow. In the census her daughter's occupation was given as 'Domestic Nurse'. She presumably helped with the children in the school which would have been run more on the lines of a nursery and held in Sarah's house in Southgate. Dame schools could quickly come and go, and *Bulmer's* mentions one in Market Place run by Mrs. Ombler Russell, although she does not feature in the census of a year earlier. In the newer and more upper-class part of town, 44-year-old Miss Letitia Stone taught music and painting, most probably out of normal school hours, at her mother's house in Eastbourne Road.

Hornsea had five day schools run by qualified people. Three of them also took boarders. Their presence is explained by the fact that quite a few well-to-do Hull businessmen had moved residence to Hornsea. They probably wanted an education for their children better than that provided by the ordinary village school. To serve their needs enterprising teachers had set up private institutions in the town. Withernsea, another sea-side town attracting commuters from Hull, similarly had private academies in addition to the ordinary village school. At Hornsea the boarding schools provided not only for the children of residents but also for children from much farther afield. In Grosvenor Terrace, Mary Skinner's high school for

---

Southfield House,

HIGH SCHOOL for GIRLS

PRINCIPAL:
Miss Mary Skinner,

Assisted by highly Qualified resident & visiting Staff.

TENNIS, GYMNASIUM, SCHOOL LIBRARY.

Terms on application.

Miss Skinner's High School for Girls advertised in Fretwell's Guide to Hornsea, *1894. There were five pupils boarding there on the eve of the census in 1891: two girls born in the West Indies, two born in Kent and one in Durham.*

Miss Skinner's school (the house with the tower) as it is today.

girls had boarders born in the Colonies as well as others born in Kent and Durham. Their parents were probably working or serving abroad.

At Henry Elsom's classical and commercial school for boys, at Holly Lodge (now Cusworth's shop) in Newbegin, there were three boarders on census day. One was from Hull and two were from Cottingham. Five years later Elsom was to move his school to the newly built St. Bede's on Atwick Road. There were then about 60 pupils, including termly and weekly boarders and day boys from Hornsea and the villages around. Saint Bede's produced some notable personalities including Sir Brian Rix, the actor, and Harold Loten. The latter became Sheriff of Hull in 1944 and was awarded the M.B.E. for services to the public in 1950. He was the son of Arthur Loten the chemist, who in 1891 had his shop (still a chemist's) at the junction of Newbegin and Cliff Road. At that time Harold was aged three. He joined Henry Elsom's school immediately on its moving to its new site at St. Bede's.

At Leylands School on Atwick Road, where the principal was John Bull Ridges, there were six boarders in 1891, mostly originating from Hull. From the age of the boarders it would seem that both Holly Lodge and Leylands provided for boys up to the age of 14 or 15. At Miss Skinner's there were two boarders aged 16 and one aged 17.

In the census return practically every child between the ages of four and thirteen is described as 'Scholar'. The great majority of them attended the National Schools, either the Infants' or the Mixed. Children began their school days at the Infants', some at the age of three. The youngest child enrolled in 1891 was Emily Clarke aged two years and three months. When the children had reached the necessary standard they were sent on to the Mixed School. However, overcrowding sometimes compelled the

Holly Lodge today.

Holly Lodge, Hornsea.

Day and Boarding School
For BOYS.

A Thorough Education given to each Pupil.

Special Attention given to Commercial Subjects.

ARITHMETIC, SHORTHAND, WRITING, BOOK-KEEPING, &c.

Gymnasium, Playground, Cricket & Football Fields.

Fully Equipped Workshop for Technical Instruction.

Inspection Invited.

Terms, References, and Successes upon Application.

Principal, H. ELSOM (Lond. Univ.)
First-class Trained Certificated Teacher; Certified Teacher of Science and Art; late Student of the Guild and School of Handicraft, London.

Henry Elsom's school advertised in Fretwell's Guide. *Four boarders were in residence on census day.*

In 1896 Henry Elsom moved his school to the newly built St. Bede's in Atwick Road.

mistress to send the children on early. In 1888 she recorded that all the six-year-olds had been sent to the Mixed School. It was not long before some of them were sent back because they did not come up to standard. Overcrowding was a problem. The Infants' School consisted of only two class-rooms, one just over 25 foot long by 20 foot wide, and the other 18 foot long by 11 foot wide. Fortunately, the larger class-room was very high (24 foot) which enabled a gallery to be built at one end. In 1891 the school inspector was recommending that the open sides of the seats in the gallery should be protected by a rail. In all, the school was supposed to accommodate 65 pupils, but when this was the actual attendance being reached in 1894, the school inspector wrote, 'The school is overcrowded; were the attendance less irregular it would also be understaffed' — a hint to the managers to take on an extra teacher. The hint was taken, and two months later the master of the Mixed School recorded in the school log book that an extra teacher, Miss Eva Bone, was to commence at the Infants' School: 'We shall not now be compelled to take them from that school before they are ready, as Miss Bone will count for an average of 30.'

For the first three-quarters of the 19th century schooling was not compulsory. The schools that did exist received no state aid until after 1833 when Government grants to voluntary schools became available. Before that, however, the different religious denominations had begun to take an active interest in education, and the Church of England established the National Society to help with the building of schools and the provision of equipment. The Nonconformist bodies established the British Society for the same purpose. Both the Hornsea Infants' and Mixed Schools, built in the 1840s, were National Schools and came under the aegis of the Church of England. They were entitled to the Government grant on the usual condition that they underwent annual inspection by Her Majesty's Inspector.

The Education Act of 1870 required that if the school accommodation provided by the voluntary bodies was inadequate then a school board was to be elected by the ratepayers who could establish a rate-aided board school. Any religious instruction given in the board schools was to be undenominational.

Hornsea, however, seems to have been happy with its National Schools. There was no demand for another school (for one thing, it would have meant an addition to the rates) and the vicar continued to make his morning visit to the Mixed School, taking the upper standards in Scripture. After 1870, however, H.M. Inspector no longer tested the children for religious knowledge. If required, this was carried out by the Diocesan Inspector. Consequently, the children of Hornsea faced two tests a year, one from H.M. Inspector and one from the Diocesan Inspector.

Although Hornsea had no need to establish a school board in order to provide extra school buildings, it did, as allowed by the 1870 Act, establish one in 1884 in order to enforce attendance at the existing National Schools. The board was elected by the Hornsea ratepayers and was therefore not necessarily completely Anglican in its composition. In 1892 its five members included Thomas Holmes, a Wesleyan, and Joseph Wade, a churchwarden at St. Nicholas church from 1879 to 1882 but who had declined re-election in 1883 'because he wished to be at liberty to attend whatever place of worship he chose'. Despite the Nonconformist element on the board, there does not appear to have been any conflict, either between members of the board or between the board and the vicar, Mr. Tew, who, with his family, participated greatly in school affairs. Holmes's interest was most probably purely educational: he had been a member of the Hull School Board before taking up residence in Hornsea and had taken an active part in the promotion of technical education in Hull.

Serving the board were a clerk and an attendance officer who, in 1892, were John Ridges and A. H. Scholefield, principal and assistant master, respectively, at Leylands private school. It was not unusual for schoolteachers to take extra jobs in order to supplement what could be fairly meagre incomes. It was the attendance officer's job to follow up any reports of non-attendance reported by the master of the National School. Parents could be fined at the magistrates' court if their children were absent from school without reasonable excuse.

Poor attendance was a source of great worry to the master, not least because his income depended largely on the numbers at school. When George Milner was appointed master in 1870 his income

The National Mixed School on Mereside was erected in 1845.

was made up of a guaranteed £40 a year, together with the school pence paid by the children, and half the annual grant received by the school from the Government. At that time, the average annual attendance was approaching 100, with the children paying, on average, threepence a week, equivalent to about 50p a year. The Government grant amounted to approximately £120. This meant that over two-thirds of the master's income came from the school pence and the grant. At the beginning of 1891, the fees for most of the children were threepence a week, with those in the higher standards paying fourpence. In January 1890 the board had decided that 'really poor parents' were to pay only twopence a week for their children's education. The Government grant was based on the average attendance for the year and the performance of the children at the annual examination by H.M. Inspector. Consequently, keeping up the attendance and preparing the children for the visit of H.M.I. were the abiding concerns of the master of the school. This applied even after 1 September 1891, when school fees were at last abolished by Parliament and primary education was made free; the loss of the school pence was made up by increasing the grant, which still depended on attendance and performance in the examination. The following entries in the school log book by George Milner's successor, Isaac Gilman, master from 1888 to 1897, will therefore need no explanation.

'Feb. 21st, 1890. The parents of Samuel Jackson, Louisa Atkin and Annie Evans were each fined 5/- [25p] at Leven on Wednesday for irregularity.

'Mar. 7th. The prosecutions, mentioned on the last page, have produced a more satisfactory state of things as far as attendance is concerned.

'June 13th. Had 193 present on 2 mornings this week. Promised the children that the first time we get 200 present we shall leave school a little earlier & have some sports on the Green. They have tried very hard to bring their absent comrades to school.

'July 18th. Punished several boys for truancy.

'July 25th. The attendance in the afternoons is better since I punished some for playing on the sands *etc.*

'Oct. 31st. Bought a new foot-ball for the boys for 5/6 [27½p], the result being an extraordinary increase in attendance.

'Dec. 12th. Gave a Christmas Card to each of the 8 best children (3 Rs only) in the first five standards, & to all present in Sts. VI-VII.

'Jan. 3rd, 1891. A list of the 8 best in each Class appeared in the *Hornsea Gazette.*

'Feb. 6th. The 'green' is now dry enough for football. By announcing that we should play today at noon & after school at night, the no. present this afternoon was the greatest we have had for a long time.

'Nov. 25th (Wed). Have not had less than 180 present this week, so far. The boys have football every time there are 180 present.

'Aug. 19th, 1892. Closed at noon for 5 weeks' holiday. The Harvest will not be commenced for another fortnight, but the Master & Managers thought that this was the best time to close, as this is the busy time for visitors and lodging house keepers.

'Sep. 30th (Fri). Holiday in afternoon to prevent lowering of average. [The harvest was still keeping boys away from school.]

'Oct. 9th (Mon). Ascertained that many children are going to Hull Fair on Wedy. so have decided to have a holiday on that day.

'Feb. 23rd, 1894. The St. 3 Grammar is so bad, that there will have to be a lesson in it twice daily until the Examn.

'Mar. 27th. Told the children that the most regular boy and girl for the year will receive a Waterbury watch each, the others to have books and certificates as in former years. Announced also that next year, ending March 31/95, the 3 best (most regular and punctual) boys and 3 best girls will receive Waterbury watches.

'Dec. 26th (Sat). The 6 top children in each Standard have the pleasure of seeing their names in both the local papers today. Of course they have known of this for some time past & have worked hard in consequence.'

These entries, and many like them, show that Isaac Gilman more often employed the carrot than the stick. It may not have been the best thing for discipline: following a poor report from H.M.I. in 1894, 'the worst the School has received since 1870', the managers felt that 'They entirely concur in the opinion of the Inspector as expressed to the Vicar, "That the want of discipline is at the bottom of this grievous failure." They think that Mr. Gilman cannot be aware how widely spread is the dissatisfaction among the parents at his lack of method and order, and they are the more surprised that so far from taking steps to remedy this defect he has allowed it to go to such lengths as to incur the severe rebuke of H.M. Inspector, although he has been again and again remonstrated with by the Vicar...'. In the next three years the Inspector's reports were better, but after Gilman resigned in 1897 there was still criticism to come from his successor, Herbert Sykes. In September 1897, in almost his first entry in the log book, Sykes criticized the lack of order and discipline at the school and wrote, 'The boys have not been accustomed to assemble in the yard but to come in indiscriminately, some of them smoking [clay pipes] until they are quite near the school doors, then swaggering in, whistling on the way.'

The efforts of Gilman, the attendance officer and the magistrates, coupled with the fact that Hornsea's population was increasing, meant that the average attendance at the school improved over the years. For the year ending April 1891 it was 165, and the Government grant amounted to £141 18s 6d. We do not know whether Isaac Gilman was engaged on the same terms as his predecessor but, if he was, he would have had the quite appreciable income of about £150.

The school log books (there was a separate one for the Infants' school), besides giving an account of events at the schools, give a fascinating insight into life in Hornsea, and references to them will be found elsewhere in these pages. There were far fewer school holidays then than there are now. The children were usually due back on January 1st after the Christmas holiday, they had the usual Bank Holidays off, but no more than the Good Friday and the Bank Holiday at Easter, and only five weeks for summer. They did, however, have a week's holiday after the visit of H.M.I., with staff and pupils no doubt near a state of collapse. The summer holiday was usually timed to begin with the harvest, so that children could help in the fields, but 1891 was the last year that this happened at Hornsea. The school board then decided that the holiday should begin earlier and coincide more with the seaside season, as more children were drawn away by that than by the harvest.

The lack of long holidays was partially offset by the number of half-days given for local social events. Beside the holiday for Hull Fair, already mentioned, there were half days and days for such occasions as the Agricultural Show, the Primitives' Sunday School tea, the Wesleyans' and Anglicans' school treats, the 'Band of Hope' outing, the Hornsea hirings and the Druids Friendly Society club feast. The presence of Ginnett's Circus on the Green in September 1893 was another occasion for a holiday. In June 1887 the children had a whole week's holiday to celebrate Queen Victoria's Jubilee. As Mr. Gilman's contract also included serving as church organist and choir master, there was also the occasional half-day holiday if he and the choir boys had to be present at a wedding during the week. Holidays were sometimes enforced by bad weather and epidemics, if for no other reason than to keep up the official average attendance on which the vital Government grant depended.

Whatever Isaac Gilman's salary was, he earned it.

The classes were large and, by today's standards, the school was seriously understaffed. In 1894, for instance, there were 78 children in the junior room in charge of an assistant teacher, Miss Kate Marshall, and a monitress, Augusta Sedman. In the senior room, Isaac Gilman and Beatrice Buttimer, a second-year pupil teacher, were in charge of 83 pupils. Twenty-year-old Miss Emma Stephenson, assistant teacher and sewing mistress, had charge of 51 children in the class room. Besides supervising the school and his largely inexperienced staff, Gilman had the task of teaching Walter Jackson, a 14-year-old first-year pupil teacher, the rudiments of his intended profession. If ever the 212 pupils had all put in an appearance at the same time, there was a total of 271 feet of benches to sit on and 185 feet of desk space for them to work at. Fortunately, the lower forms used slates for writing on, and a desk was not essential. Gilman was not always blessed with enthusiastic staff. Augusta Sedman occasionally needed a day off to recover from a night in Hull, and in 1892 Gilman had to record in the log book that Miss Crowe read newspapers in school hours, continually allowed children to leave early and did not begin lessons until ten or 15 minutes after the other classes. As a result, Standard II was doing very badly. Perhaps worst of all for Gilman was that he seldom had the reward of his brightest pupils staying on until the end of their school careers and helping to raise the standard at the annual visit of H.M.I., as the following entry from the log book shows:

'Nov. 8th, 1895. Very much annoyed at losing another of my best scholars — Ellen Stephenson (St. 6) who could do all her work well. She has gone to Miss Skinner's Ladies' School to be "finished off" as her father informs me. I need hardly say that these Middle & Upper class schools take many of our best children. Three new schools have opened during the last few years — Miss Dabb's, Mr. Elsom's & Mrs. Thom's.' [Ellen Stephenson, who was aged seven on the day of the census in 1891, was the daughter of a grocer in Southgate. Miss Dabb's and Mrs. Thom's schools had both come into existence since 1892.]

In 1897, when the average attendance for the year was down on the previous year, Gilman ascribed it partially to 'the opening of several new private schools which take practically all the better class children (Last year my 2 best girls went to Miss Skinner's, & several boys to Mr. Elsom's Commercial School).'

With often poor support from his staff, the loss of his best pupils, and criticism from the managers, parents and the vicar Gilman no doubt thought it was time to go, and on 3 June 1897 entered in the log, 'Gave notice to the managers that I should resign my duties here on Aug. 31st.' His last entry was on 30 July: 'Closed for the Summer Holiday. As this is my last day at school, several children gave me some nice presents.' Life was not all bad.

BURTON CONSTABLE HALL

Home of the
Lord Paramount of the Seigniory of Holderness

A magnificent 16th century home with outstanding 18th century additions.

Collections Include:
Paintings, Chippendale Furniture and unique exhibition of 18th century scientific instruments

Opening from Easter until the end of September each Sunday to Thursday

The grounds open at 12 noon and the Hall from 1 pm until 4.30 pm

We have a Coffee Shop and free car park

A DAY OUT WITH A DIFFERENCE

Butterfly World

Attractions

Food & Restaurant

Hornsea has changed! As well as the Yorkshire Car Collection, Birds of Prey and Adventure Playground we've a whole new shopping experience. The Hornsea Freeport Shopping Village. Offering top brands at discount prices. Shops include Laura Ashley, Alexon, Dash, Wrangler, Austin Reed, and Aquascutum. Our famous Factory Shop sells chain store seconds and end of ranges - all at low, low prices. Hornsea Pottery's world renowned tableware is also available. The Yorkshire Car Collection - an exciting display of veteran, vintage and classic cars. Parking and site admission are free

Fashion

Pottery

FREEDOM PASS
All five attractions for just
£3.99
Great Value
*Reduced rates for children & O.A.P's

THE YORKSHIRE CAR COLLECTION at Hornsea Pottery

HORNSEA FREEPORT shopping village

HORNSEA POTTERY LEISURE PARK

Member of Peter Black   VISA   HORNSEA POTTERY HORNSEA YORKSHIRE HU18 IUT TEL:0964 534211

9 — Public Services

When the enumerator called at 'The Waterworks' in Atwick Road to take the census in 1891 his mind perhaps went back to the days before 1879 when Hornsea had to rely on water from pumps and wells — much of which was declared to be 'less than wholesome' — and to the task of obtaining a good supply which had proved both lengthy and difficult. Now, he might have reflected, since the completion of the Waterworks, a supply of pure drinking water was available to all customers at the turn of a tap. In this respect, Hornsea was unique amongst the villages of Holderness.

The house at the Waterworks was occupied by the engineer, John Holme, and his wife and daughter. It was John Holme who was responsible to the Hornsea Local Board of Health which had been formed in 1864. He had also been responsible to the consultants appointed by the Board to plan and oversee the construction of the plant and piping and subsequent operation. The provision of a good water supply was just one of the Board's achievements during the 31 years of its existence.

England's population had risen greatly in the 19th century, more especially in the expanding industrial areas. This led to poor housing, lack of a safe water supply and bad sanitation. Not surprisingly, this in turn led to widespread epidemics bringing in their wake death and illness on scales not encountered since the plagues of the 17th century.

After a number of cholera epidemics in the middle of the century the Government, amid widespread fear and concern, enacted legislation which enabled local health boards to be established whose responsibilities would include the fight against disease. The principal legislation was contained in the Local Government Act of 1858. Subsequent legislation included the Public Health Act of 1875 which laid down in broad terms the duties and responsibilities of the various existing bodies and made provision for the formation of others. These local bodies were able to finance projects by way of Government loans and the setting of local rates to repay such expenditure.

The Local Government Act of 1858 enabled local health boards to be set up subject to the approval of the Secretary of State. It was envisaged that the functions of the boards would include the provision of a safe water supply, the provision of an efficient drainage and sewerage system, refuse removal, maintenance of roads and footpaths, provision of street lighting if necessary, the provision of land for burials, and the cleansing of houses, work places and schools in which persons suffering from notifiable diseases were living or working.

Many of the problems which led to the Government's action were restricted to the great towns, particularly the rapidly developing industrial cities, and did not exist to any degree in Hornsea. Nevertheless, the town possessed neither a piped water supply nor a deep drainage system and, for those who wished to see the development of Hornsea as both a residential town and a seaside resort, such improvements were considered an essential element in the achievement of their aims. By 1862, the intended developers had already paved the way for better access to the town by obtaining an Act to build a railway from Hull to Hornsea. Using the recommendations of the 1858 Act, they continued to further their aims by calling a meeting of property owners and rate-payers to consider the establishment of a local board of health. The meeting took place on 19 November 1863, and by a majority of 39 votes to 31 it was decided to put the matter to all residents. A public meeting was held on 23 December 1863 under the chairmanship of Joseph Armytage Wade. Already chairman of the Hull and Hornsea Railway

Hornsea House, Eastgate, the home of Joseph Armytage Wade, the man who had much to do with the formation of the Hornsea Local Board of Health in 1864. The house was later occupied by Christopher Pickering.

The lodge to Hornsea House still stands at the entrance to the school which was built on the site of the house.

The Ley Hill waterworks. In 1891 the adjoining house was occupied by waterworks engineer, John Holme.

Company, he was to become chairman of the Hornsea Gas Light and Coke Company when it was formed in 1866. He was the driving force in the development of Hornsea, and the establishment of a local board of health can be seen as an essential factor in achieving his objective. The meeting approved the proposal that the Hornsea Local Board of Health be formed, subject to the approval of the Secretary of State.

The necessary approval was obtained along with the authority for the Board to levy a rate on local residents to cover the cost of projects undertaken. The Board's inaugural meeting was held on 5 May 1864. Six weeks previously, the Hull and Hornsea railway line had been opened. Stirring times, indeed, for Hornsea!

At the inaugural meeting Wade was voted in as chairman and, together with 11 other residents, formed the Board. The aims and priorities were identified and a number of committees were established with responsibilities for Waterworks, Highways, Burial and Sanitation. A sub-committee was also given the responsibility for Street Lighting. A young farmer, Thomas Hornsey of Hornsea Burton, was appointed as the Board's first clerk. (He went on to be the first clerk to the Hornsea Urban District Council when it was formed 31 years later.) It was resolved that the first priority should be given to the provision of a safe water supply together with the construction of a deep drainage and sewerage system.

The Board was to spend a number of years in planning exactly what should be done but for a while no real progress was made. Then, in 1874, a Government inspector visited the town. In his report to the Home Office, he indicated what everyone already knew — that the water being drawn from pumps and wells was 'less than wholesome' and represented 'a hazard to public health'. He concluded that 'the construction of a waterworks and the provision of a piped water system were a critical necessity'.

Stung into action by the report, the Board made an application to the Public Works Loan Board for a loan of £20,000 to enable work to proceed without delay. The money was to be repaid over the next 30 years through a rate charged on all local residents.

The application was approved, detailed plans were

drawn up and a suitable site on Leys Hill on Atwick Road was acquired. Water of good quality was found after test borings which went 265 feet below the surface and passed through 128 feet of solid chalk.

An engine house was constructed to house the powerful engines used to draw the water to the surface. The two most visible buildings were the water tower, 98 foot higher than the level of the town, and the chimney, over 100 foot high, designed to carry engine fumes away from the tower. The tower could store 56,000 gallons of water, which, in 1891, was enough to supply the town for one day. Situated a mile from the town centre, the Victorian building still stands as a tribute to its builders although today it serves as a 'Civic amenity site' where residents may dispose of unwanted refuse. The former engineer's house has recently been converted into three flats, providing temporary accommodation for homeless people.

The water was passed through a series of filters and aerated to give it 'sparkle'. Tests for purity were carried out on a continuing basis by the staff at the waterworks and samples were sent daily to the Medical Officer of Health for analysis.

In 1877, while the piping to the town had yet to be completed, the Medical Officer of Health reported that the water coming from the wells and pumps in the town was unfit to drink. As an interim measure, John Holme, the waterworks engineer, came up with the idea of using a water-cart to supply water direct from the waterworks to householders at a cost of a halfpenny (0.2p) for a four-gallon bucket. Even after the piped system had been completed this service was to continue to a small number of houses located outside the area covered by the piped supply.

The waterworks and the pipes to supply the majority of houses in the town became operational in 1879. The cost had been £9,652.

Notwithstanding the undoubted purity of the water, local residents continued to complain about its 'hardness'. In 1891 a large number of houses still had pumps in their backyards. Here the water came either from shallow wells, well above the chalk layer, or from cisterns taking the water off the roofs of the houses. In both cases, the water was 'soft' and the housewives no doubt considered it far better than Leys Hill water for getting a lather, particularly when washing clothes and hair. Complaints about hard water continued throughout the working life of the Leys Hill waterworks which, as the town expanded, took water from extra bore-holes, one nearer the town, but still in Atwick Road, and the other south of Bewholme Lane, from where the water was piped to Leys Hill.

At the same time as work was being carried out to bring a safe water supply to the houses in the town, a deep drainage and sewerage system was being constructed at a cost of £10,000. The project involved the laborious construction of brick sewers, all the digging being by hand and the sewers being built *in situ* by bricklayers. The sewers enabled surface water to be drained from the roads by way of a series of gullies and gratings. Prior to this the streets could quickly turn to a quagmire after a rainstorm, and a walk through Hornsea could be both difficult and unpleasant. Foot-scrapers by the doorways of old houses testify to the state the footpaths could be in.

The new system also provided for the removal of waste water and sewage from homes in the town. Prior to this, most houses relied on a 'soakaway' to remove water used for washing and cooking, sometimes leading to the contamination of drinking water pumped up from shallow wells. Domestic sewage was held in cesspits until it could be cleared and collected periodically by 'nightsoil men' during the hours of darkness. The product found a ready market with the farmers, who used it as fertiliser.

Very few flush toilets were in existence at the beginning of the 20th century; indeed, until the provision of a piped-water system they were not a practical option. A 'petty' or 'closet', usually located at the bottom of the garden, was the more usual arrangement. Very few houses had a bathroom, and baths were usually taken, seldom more often than weekly, in front of the fire in the kitchen, the water often being used by more than one member of the family.

With the advent of piped water and deep drainage, indoor flush toilets could be more easily provided and bathrooms constructed. Newer houses tended to have such facilities, as well as water on tap in the kitchen, built-in, whilst over the years older properties were adapted to provide such services. It was probably because these possibilities existed that wealthy people began to take up residence in Hornsea in preference to some of the old-established, but more primitive, residential areas to the west of Hull.

From its inception in 1864 until superseded by the Hornsea Urban District Council in 1895 the Local Board of Health was responsible for the roads and footpaths in the town. In 1891 the motor car had still to make its appearance on the roads of the East Riding. The traffic was almost exclusively horse drawn, with only the occasional hand-cart, cycle and steam-propelled traction engine to be seen. The best that could be expected of the local roads was that they would be regularly treated with a top dressing of rolled gravel or broken stones. In winter the roads became rutted with the passing of heavy iron-wheeled carts, particularly steam traction engines towing threshing machines from farm to farm. Summertime brought its own problems — dry weather caused the roads to become very dusty, and in the built-up areas a water cart fitted with a sprinkler would be sent round at frequent intervals to water the roads. Horses, pulling vehicles of all kinds, and cows being driven from fields to milking sheds and back, brought their own problems, and frequent sweeping of the roads was necessary throughout the year.

The footpaths were in the main paved with rolled

This view west along Newbegin gives an indication of the state of the streets at the turn of the century. Note the raised causeway in the foreground, allowing women to keep their long dresses reasonably clean when crossing the street. From the right, the buildings are Loten's chemist's shop (still a chemist's), Loten's plumber's, the Public Rooms (on the site of the present library), the Wesleyan Methodist chapel and the Wesleyan Sunday school.

gravel, although in the town centre flag-stones were beginning to appear. Ladies' long dresses and coats made a walk through the streets or along the sea front a hazardous experience which was only slightly eased by the daily sweeping of the paths. To help keep long clothing clean when crossing the roads, there were raised causeways across some of the streets.

Tarred granite chippings were to appear on main streets before 1914, but the transformation of roads to modern standards did not commence until the 1920s when motor traffic began to increase. Today's traffic loads are much higher than could have been envisaged in the days of the Local Board. Despite many improvements, the roads still remain far from perfect and are never 'completed' to everyone's satisfaction.

Street lighting was paid for out of the rates levied by the Local Board of Health. In the 1890s gas for the lamps was obtained from two companies — the Hornsea Gas Light and Coke Company and the Lansdowne Gas Company. The former company had been formed as far back as 1866. It had a share capital of £3,000 raised mainly by local people purchasing shares at £2 10s (£2.50). The chairman was Joseph Wade. The company secretary was Thomas Hornsey, the clerk to the Board of Health. The works, which were managed by Thomas Cope in 1891, were built on land adjacent to the goods yard of the Hornsea Bridge railway station. From there it was possible for the coal for the plant to be shunted on rail-wagons directly to the furnace. The process produced not only gas, but also creosote and various specialist oils, all of which found a ready market in the expanding industries of those times. The gas was stored in a massive gas holder which formed a prominent landmark along with the nearby chimney of Wade's Hornsea Brick and Tile Works. From the holder the gas was distributed by a system of underground lead pipes. In the 1890s the works supplied 49 of the public street lamps in Hornsea as well as most of the houses requiring gas.

The rival concern, the Lansdowne gasworks, was located on the site of a former gravel pit at the rear of Fairfield House on Cliff Lane (now Cliff Road). Access to the site was via Hartley Street. The company supplied a number of homes to the north of the town as well as eight public street lights in the same area.

At dusk each evening the public lights were lit by the town's two lamp-lighters. Carrying short ladders, they went round to each lamp in turn and lit it with a match. It was not until the early 1930s, when the gas company had to compete with the electricity suppliers for the contract, that the gas lamps were fitted with by-pass pilot lights. This meant that the lamps could be lit simply by opening the valve using a long pole with a hook on the end. Hornsea's last two lamp-lighters were Mr. 'Zeppelin Jack' Bradley (so-called because of his watchman duties in the First World War) and Mr. Kennedy. Before the introduction of the by-pass valves, they each used two boxes of matches during their nightly round. Obviously, by that time there were far more street lamps than there had been in 1891.

Gas supplies to houses, shops and other users terminated at a meter just inside the premises. The meter either recorded the amount of gas used, for which an account was rendered, or was operated by a coin in the slot (either one old penny or a shilling). The owner or occupier was responsible for the provision of pipes within the property. Often the supply was limited to providing lights in the principal rooms on the ground floor, the remainder being lit by either oil lamps or candles. In some houses, particularly rented properties, where the owner was not prepared to meet the cost of installation, or where the resident was fearful of an explosion, it was many years before gas was provided, and the old methods of lighting continued. Hornsea, of course, was expanding rapidly at this time and, as new houses were being built, the builders were more lavish in the distribution of gas to different parts of the house, not only taking it to the bedrooms for lighting but also to the kitchens to supply gas rings.

Local boards of health were responsible for providing cemeteries when church graveyards became full. Despite the fact that Hornsea had a Burial Committee, the main Board was extremely loath to inflict an extra rate on the residents by the purchase of land, although it was apparent that St. Nicholas churchyard was overflowing. However, in 1873 the newly appointed vicar, Edmund Tew, showed great concern about the state of his churchyard: it was full, it was insanitary and it was unsightly. He contacted the Local Board and the matter was discussed at length. While some members were prepared to make public funds available for a new cemetery, others, including the chairman, Joseph Wade, thought that other avenues should be explored before committing funds to what would be a costly project. Large sums were already being borrowed to finance the waterworks and sewerage schemes. Not satisfied, the vicar made representations to the Government through Church channels and, following intervention by the Secretary of State, the Local Health Board agreed to make land available. The first site considered was on land adjacent to the proposed waterworks on Ley Hill! After some controversy the idea of that site was abandoned and eventually a site was purchased off Southgate, where a mortuary chapel and a board room, from which the the Local Board could conduct its business, were constructed. The new cemetery was opened in 1885, the whole cost being £1,600. Lewis Landermore was appointed as keeper and in 1891 he and his wife were living in a two-roomed house close to the cemetery. With the opening of the cemetery the churchyard was closed for burials, except for those cases where family vaults existed, Joseph Wade himself being buried in the Wade vault in 1896.

Thus, by the 1890s the Hornsea Local Board of Health had achieved many of its aims. Besides providing a supply of clean water and a proper

The mortuary chapel and board room at the entrance to the cemetery in Southgate.

sewerage system, it had also provided a new cemetery, organized a weekly refuse collection, and arranged for roads and footpaths to be regularly cleaned, maintained and lit. Not all these objectives were achieved without much heated discussion, local objections and sometimes Government intervention but, during a period of expansion, the Board's achievements were considerable. However, it may be that the Board's reluctance to impose higher rates on Hornsea property-owners was justifiable. There seems to have been a considerable fall in the number of people moving to take up residence in Hornsea after most of the schemes were completed. In the decade that the railway came (1861-71) Hornsea's population went up by 622, a rise of nearly 60%. In the next two decades the rise was only 19%. It is interesting to note that at Withernsea, lower down the coast and also connected to Hull by rail, the increase in population between 1871 and 1891 was greater than Hornsea's in terms of numbers, being 358 compared with 328 at Hornsea. In percentage terms the increase was far greater, being 55% in the 20 years compared with Hornsea's 19%. One big difference between the two resorts was that Withernsea was still only part of a rural sanitary authority (it did not have its own local board of health) and relied mostly on open ditches to deal with its sewage. The town was to have no piped water supply until 1916. The rates at Withernsea must have been far lower than at Hornsea. Hull commuters wishing to live by the sea seem to have been more prepared to put up with Withernsea's primitive sanitation than to pay Hornsea's high rates. Those who did choose Hornsea were probably the better-off — perhaps, one more factor contributing to Hornsea's well-known air of reserve.

HOLIDAYS

for the complete travel service contact

Holderness TRAVEL LTD

ABTA 35014

2 New Road, Hornsea
Tel: 533315/532671

For a fast and friendly service Est 1965

Excellence in Furnishing in East Yorkshire

The very best in carpets, vinyl and soft furnishings as well as upholstery

All time served craftsmen and women produce the finest results in your home and in our own workshops

Blinds - Beds - Suites - Honey Pine - Buckingham Dining - Contract - Commercial - Ships - Rigs - Homes

Hornsea Furnishing Co.

4-6 New Road, Hornsea. Tel: (0964) 532929

Do you have any questions about banking we can help answer?

YES ☐   **YES** ☐

TSB
**We want YOU
to say YES**

TSB Bank plc, 20 Newbegin, Hornsea, North Humberside HU18 1AG.
Telephone: 0964 532102.

GEORGE HAMPSON
ELECTRICAL & LIGHTING

- SMALL ELECTRICAL APPLIANCES
- LIGHTING DEPT.
- HOUSEWARES AND KITCHENWARE
- VACUUM CLEANERS WASHING MACHINE SALES
- SERVICE & REPAIRS — Hoover Washing Machines, Tumble Driers, Twin Tubs, Dishwashers, Vacuum Cleaners, etc.

34 NEWBEGIN, HORNSEA
TEL: (0964) 535652

For an expert shoe repair, key cutting and sharpening service for knives, shears, scissors and lawn mowers

All promptly carried out to your satisfaction

HEEL AND KEY BAR
118 NEWBEGIN HORNSEA. 536253

Household and Kitchen wares
Always an excellent selection in stock at very competitive prices

---

J. B. ROBINSON,
NEWSAGENT,
Tobacconist, Confectioner, &c.,
NEWBEGIN HOUSE,
NEWBEGIN, HORNSEA.

Magazines, Periodicals, Weekly and Daily Papers regularly supplied.

Agent for the "HORNSEA GAZETTE."

The above advertisement appeared in the Hornsea Guide for 1894.
It could have been written today --
The shop where value, service and civility have passed the test of time.

IMAGES
FAST EFFICIENT PHOTO PROCESSING

24 HOUR SERVICE

* Cameras * Films * Batteries
* Frames * Camera Accessories
* Wedding Photography
* Passport ID Photographs

27 NEWBEGIN, HORNSEA
Tel: Hornsea 535980

10 — Communications

In 1892, *Bulmer's Directory* recorded that Hornsea had a town crier, one Aaron Usher, whose office survived from the time when most people received news and ideas by word of mouth. To us, in 1993, a town crier is but a tourist attraction and must have seemed quaint to many even in 1892. During the 1860s over 20% of the brides and grooms in the East Riding were unable to sign the marriage registers and had to make a mark instead. In 1868 the vicar of Hornsea, referring to the pupils at the National School on Mereside, said, 'They for the most part soon forget all they have learned at school, and when they come to be married cannot write their own names.' Though the figure for illiteracy had fallen to 3% in the 1890s, there would still have been a fair proportion of old people lacking the ability to read newspapers and books. For these people the town crier may still have had a real value, especially in notifying them of such events as public meetings or forthcoming elections.

For those who could read, newspapers were easily available, and cheap. Hornsea's own weekly, the *Hornsea Gazette*, cost one penny. In 1896 Alfred Harmsworth brought out the *Daily Mail*, the first national newspaper to retail at a halfpenny. The national newspapers were distributed quickly by rail, and Hornsea had three newsagencies, though each was part of other businesses. William Robinson, newsagent in Southgate, was also a boot and shoe maker, Mrs. Henderson in Market Place was a grocer, and James Robinson of Newbegin House was a grocer, confectioner and tobacconist. Newspapers were also available from the W. H. Smith bookstall at the railway station.

Newspaper circulation had increased greatly after the stamp-duty on newspapers was finally removed in 1855, and the power of the press was developing with the spread of literacy and easy transport. Thanks to the railways, national news could be read in Hornsea within 12 hours of it being published in Fleet Street, a far cry from the days earlier in the century

Cook Laking's advertisement in Fretwell's Guide to Hornsea *refers to the picture postcards of Hornsea that are for sale.*

COOK LAKING,

General Draper, Hosier,

and Haberdasher.

Sole Agent for sale of Poulton & Son's Artistic Views of Hornsea.

Agent for PULLAR and SONS, Dyers to the Queen, Perth.

Depot of the Society for promoting Christian Knowledge.

Newbegin, HORNSEA.

when newspapers were sent by coach and the London to York journey took four days. One can imagine the changed situation in the 1890s, when the businessman, commuting between Hull and Hornsea, could pick up his *Times* or his *Telegraph* at W. H. Smith's and study the financial pages in the train on his way to work. Hornsea had certainly lost whatever isolation it may have once had due to the difficulties of road travel.

Postal services also benefited from the use of the rail network. In Hornsea much of the mail must have originated with the visitors; postcards were already popular in 1891, although it was not until after 1894, when private cards were allowed to replace the official postcards, that picture postcards came into popular use. In 1891 the post office was in Southgate close to the junction with Newbegin. Mrs. Paulina Alman, a 54-year-old widow, was the postmistress, combining the duties with an ironmongery business. There were two deliveries of letters daily, via Hull, and three collections. There was also a collection on Sundays. In addition to the post office itself there were letter boxes in New Road and Cliff Lane (now Cliff Road) and at the railway station, although the latter did not have a Sunday collection. Helping Mrs. Alman with the mail was Charles Scott, letter carrier, who also ran a shoemaker's business in Newbegin.

The electric telegraph had come to Hornsea in 1871. The line was brought by telegraph poles along the road from Leven. In 1891 Hornsea's telegraph clerk was Annie Witty, the 22-year-old daughter of a cowkeeper in Back Southgate. She would, of course, have sent out her telegraph messages in Morse code, and her occupation represents an interesting example of the new careers that were becoming open to women at that time. She and Mrs. Alman must have worked some long hours. There are no other postal workers mentioned in the census, and the post office was open for 13 hours every weekday and for two hours on a Sunday.

The Hull and Hornsea Railway, which made possible the rapid receipt of mail and newspapers in the town, had opened in 1864. The chief promoter, and chairman of the company, was Joseph Wade. The company had only a short independent existence and by 1891 it had long been part of the network of the North Eastern Railway. The railway had attracted more residents to the town and a population of 1,063 in 1861 had increased to 2,013 by 1891. It was swelled in the season by visitors in hotels, lodging houses and rented property, and on holidays and weekends large numbers of day trippers arrived, mostly by rail. With special attractions laid on, as on August Bank holidays, the town and beach could be crowded, as reported in the *Hull Times* at the beginning of August 1892: 'The seventeenth annual regatta and aquatic sports at Hornsea were held on Monday in moderately fine weather, and the presence of an enormous influx of visitors, chiefly from Hull.'

According to the *Hornsea Gazette,* excursion trains returning from the first regatta in 1876 were kept running until two o'clock the following morning.

The change that the railway had brought to Hornsea was an established way of life by 1891. The shaping of Hornsea as a seaside resort and desirable residential town was all but complete, and the railway was an accepted and integral part of the daily life. The line was at that time a single track with as many as nine trains running each way on weekdays. On Sundays the number depended on the time of the year. The number of trains indicates plenty of traffic between Hull and Hornsea — of businessmen, shoppers, and visitors as well as freight, notably coal. For the passenger a first-class season ticket cost £12 for the year, with a second-class ticket costing £9 and a third-class £6. A day return to Hull could be had for one shilling. The slow train took 50 minutes but the express journey was done in 40 minutes. Most prudent people would allow themselves this for a journey by car to the centre of Hull today.

The railways greatly increased the mobility of

labour. By increasing the circulation and distribution of newspapers, jobs were advertised over a much wider area and people could easily move by train to a new part of the country. Mr. Henry Lewis Greenaway, who commenced his teaching duties at Hornsea School on 4 January 1888, had come from a previous post at Cirencester Church School. The correspondence, first between the school managers and the newspaper or periodical advertising the job and then between Mr. Greenaway and the school managers, would have been transported by train, as no doubt was Mr. Greenaway himself when he came to take up his new position. The birth-places of the people living in Hornsea in 1891 point to the great mobility of the population. More than 50% of Hornsea's population were born more than 10 miles from the town. The figure is far higher if only the adult population is considered.

The railway also contributed to the social life of the town and its inhabitants. Not only were Hornsea folk able to visit the theatres and music halls of Hull, but entertainment could be brought to Hornsea. The 'powerful contingent of the Hull Harmonic Society', which joined the Hornsea Congregational Church Choir to sing the *Messiah* on 3 January 1891, was typical of the interchange of choirs, soloists and musicians which took place between the two centres.

Hull's attractions were something which Isaac Gilman, the master of the Hornsea Mixed School, was always having to contend with. On 9 October 1893 he recorded in the school log book that he had 'ascertained that many children are going to Hull Fair on Wedy. so have decided to have a holiday on that day'. (By having an official holiday Mr. Gilman cut down his absenteeism figures, which affected the grant that the school received.) On 14 December 1894 he noted that 'On Tuesday nt. Augusta Sedman, the Monitress, went to a Ball in Hull, and was away from school all the following day, without leave.' The following October Miss Sedman, now a pupil teacher, was gadding again. She took a half day to go to the circus in Hull — this time with permission. Isaac Gilman no doubt regarded the railway as a mixed blessing! Augusta Sedman was a local girl, aged 14 on census day, 1891.

Hornsea's main station, which dealt chiefly with

Hornsea railway station and station-master's house. The house was far more elaborate than others along the line. In 1891 it was occupied by the station-master, William Train, his wife and seven of their children aged from 10 to 29. The three eldest sons were all railway clerks.

passengers, was presided over by the appropriately named William Train who was station-master for the last 25 years of the century. Most freight was dealt with at Hornsea Bridge station, where there were suitable off-loading facilities for the coal, fertilizers and cattle-feed which made up most of the bulky materials coming into Hornsea. There were similar facilities for handling the livestock and other agricultural products moving out. Hull's rising population created a great demand for milk, a commodity ideally suited to rail transport, which was regular, fast and reliable. By the early 1900s most stations along the Hull and Hornsea line were handling milk in churns, although it is probable that Hornsea's own considerable population could consume all the milk produced by the town's farmers and cowkeepers, especially during the holiday season.

The railway employed three agents in Hornsea in 1891. William Train, the station master, was the coal and goods agent, William Dabb was described simply as a railway agent, and Edward Hall was a carting agent. There were 16 other railway employees in Hornsea, of whom seven were clerks, mostly originating from East Riding villages, including Hornsea, and perhaps a tribute to the skill of Isaac Gilman and his like in teaching the 3 Rs.

With few exceptions, all passengers and goods by rail begin and finish their journeys by road. Hornsea's exceptions were the deliveries to the gasworks and brickworks which each had its own spur line allowing delivery of coal for the furnaces. In the case of the brickworks there may also have been direct loading of the company's products on to rail trucks, but is is more than likely that the building that went on in Hornsea itself was sufficient to absorb all the works' output, with deliveries being by horse and rully. The importance of the railway to the life and prosperity of Hornsea should not be underestimated, but it must be remembered that, then as now, the roads were the ultimate local travel and distribution system. The roads were free to all, and led everywhere, not just to Hull.

The poor walked — to work, to church, to the shops or to enjoy such social pleasures as they could afford or were free. A hawker, such as Mary Darkin, operating from her two-roomed house in Market Place, would have peddled her wares on foot. The agricultural and general labourers walked to their places of work (the price of a bicycle was not yet within the reach of their pockets) and children from all corners of the parish dragged their unwilling way to school. Other workers would have spent much of their time on the roads in the earning of their living. Cartmen, like 18-year-old Henry Norman, would have known the local roads well. The three errand boys recorded in the census, who were the final link in the chain which brought tea from India or corned beef from the Argentine, no doubt were familiar with every lane and back-street in the town.

The shopkeepers and craftsmen relied on the roads for their custom, not only from Hornsea folk but also from the people of the surrounding area wishing to purchase goods their own small communities did not supply — perhaps footwear from one of the nine boot- and shoemakers listed in Bulmer's Directory, or some potion from one of the three chemists' shops. Corn and flour dealers, coal merchants and farmers all had their wagons on the roads. Whatever is now delivered by lorry or van was then transported by horse-drawn vehicles or, in some cases. handcarts. Horses ruled the roads (although the horse population of the country as a whole was not to reach its peak of 3½ million for another 20 years) and a small army of men was needed to see to their needs and the care of the vehicles and implements they pulled. In Hornsea there were four carters, 13 grooms, a saddler, a horsebreaker, a wheelwright and three blacksmiths working in the town, as well as the wagoners and other farmworkers looking after horses on the farms. There were three cab proprietors — Dukes, Hall and Barker. Robert Barker also ran a horse-drawn bus to

C. STEPHENSON,

Wine and Spirit Merchant,

ROSE AND CROWN HOTEL,

HORNSEA.

Spirits and Cigars of the finest quality.

REFRESHMENTS PROVIDED.

GOOD STABLING.

Good Accommodation for Cyclists.

W. JOHNSON,

FASHIONABLE

BESPOKE TAILOR,

Market Place, Hornsea.

Bicycling Suits, Breeches, etc.,
Good Material, Good Fit, Good Workmanship and Style.

LADIES' COSTUMES.

Jackets in all the Newest Styles.

ULSTERS AND DOLMANS, &c.

All Orders carefully attended to.

In Bulmer's Directory *for 1892 the Rose and Crown was advertising accommodation for cyclists, and in* Fretwell's Guide *of 1894 Johnson the tailor was advertising cycling clothing for sale. In both cases the advertisements were aimed at the more well-to-do. It was to be another decade or so before the price of cycles came within a range which the working class could afford.*

Beverley from the Victoria Hotel on Saturdays at 7 a.m. In all, there were nine cab drivers, assuming the proprietors themselves drove. However, ordering a cab at the end of your stay in Hornsea would have required a walk to the proprietor's office as long as the cab journey itself or, more likely, the employment of some schoolboy truant to take a message. Not for another decade would someone in Hornsea be able to 'call a cab' by telephone as we do today.

Hornsea had three carrier services. Rose Carr in Eastgate and Edward Banks of Mereside ran carriers' carts to Hull on Tuesdays and Fridays (Hull's market days) at 6 a.m.. George Shawcross of Beeford ran a service between Hornsea and Beeford on Tuesdays. *En route* to their destinations these carriers made individual deliveries in many villages not within easy reach of the railway. In Hull such things as eggs and poultry were delivered to the market, and various purchases were made on behalf of customers in the country. Rose Carr is one of the legendary characters of Hornsea, and her career is the subject of a book by John Markham. She had arrived in Hornsea by 1872 and was recorded in *Kelly's Directory* as a carrier to Beeford. In 1891 she was 49 and living in what was indicated in the census return as a one-roomed house in Eastgate. She lived until 1913 and John Markham was able to use some 'living memory' material in his account of her life.

Roads were beginning to improve slightly at the very end of the 19th century. The pneumatic cycle tyre had been invented in the 1880s and the safety cycle, a design suitable for women cyclists, was developed soon after. Women's magazines now carried articles on cycling (usually about what dress to wear!) although it was still a pastime for the better-off. Cycling clubs began to be popular. Hornsea had its club, with Richard Webb, a wine merchant, as captain, and Charles Whiting, railway clerk and son of a Hornsea Burton farmer, as secretary. In 1892 the Rose and Crown was advertising 'Good Accommodation for Cyclists', and in 1894 Johnson's, the tailor in Market Place, could provide bicycling suits of 'Good Material, Good Fit, Good Workmanship and Style'. In 1897 there were 40 decorated cycles in the parade to celebrate Queen Victoria's Diamond Jubilee. By this time cycles could be used for delivery and no doubt the status of the errand boys improved!

The increasing popularity of the cycle at the beginning of the 20th century had the effect of reducing the passenger receipts of the railways, but it was the coming of the motor car which spelt the ultimate doom of lines like the Hull-and-Hornsea. The car made its appearance in Britain in the early nineties. With the abolition of speed limits its spread was such that by 1901 the Chief Constable of the East Riding was reporting 'receiving numerous complaints about speeding, frightening horses and destroying road surfaces'. In the course of time road surfaces, with the use of tarmacadam, became more suitable for motor vehicles, and by the 1920s there were buses and charabancs plying the roads to Hornsea. As more and more people came to own cars, rural rail-lines became uneconomical and, under the Beeching Plan, the Hull and Hornsea railway closed to passengers in 1964, just 100 years after the line had opened. The route to Hull was once again reduced to the centuries-old tortuous roads, and the direct rail route, which had played such a part in the fortunes of Hornsea, became nothing more than a bridle path.

Cammish & Company
Land & Estate Agents

Free Sales, Valuation and Marketing Advice - No obligation

★ Shared Equity ★ Part Exchange
★ Rental Purchase
★ House Buyers Chainbreaker

All innovative schemes from an estate agent who really explores every possible way to sell your home!

2 Newbegin
Hornsea HU18 1AG
Tel: 0964 534121
Fax: 0964 536638

Mary West FASHIONS

32 CLIFF ROAD, HORNSEA
Tel: (0964) 532430

BEAUTIFUL CLOTHES MILLINERY AND ACCESSORIES FOR ANY OCCASION

SIZES 8-26

CLOSED WED.   EASY PARKING

COLIN TURNER INSURANCE SERVICES

44 CLIFF ROAD
HORNSEA
HU18 1LN

INSURANCE BROKERS REGISTRATION COUNCIL — REGULATED FOR INVESTMENT BUSINESS

REGISTERED INSURANCE BROKERS

FOR ALL YOUR INSURANCE AND INVESTMENT NEEDS
MORTGAGES AND FINANCE ARRANGED

TEL AND FAX: (0964) 534907

PROMENADE HOTEL
RESIDENTIAL CARE HOME
8-10 MARINE DRIVE, HORNSEA. Tel: (0964) 533348

CARE
The Promenade Residential Care Home provides a Home for the elderly. It fosters friendship and companionship and preserves individual privacy and dignity. Our trained staff are friendly and caring providing 24 hours commitment to all residents. The home enjoys regular visits from Private/Local GP's, District Nurse, Chiropodist, Hairdressers. Convent Nuns and Priests of all denominations.

ACCOMMODATION
There are fully furnished single and double bedrooms with hand washing facilities, TV point and Nurse call system. Residents can have their own furniture if so desired. There is a large TV lounge/sitting room, dining area, a private visitors' lounge, sun porch and conservatory. To the rear of the premises there is a large garden with colourful beds and fruit trees. Car parking facilities are available for up to ten cars.

RECREATION
There is a wide variety of indoor and outdoor activities including weekly bingo, mini-bus outgoings to places of interest, garden party/barbecue, musical evenings, residents' and relatives' party, raffle and fund-raising, trips to local concerts. pantomime and theatre, etc.

CATERING
Our qualified catering staff prepares a varied menu and caters for any special dietary needs. residents can have their meals in their own rooms or in the general dining area, according to their choice.

RELATIVES AND FRIENDS
The Promenade Residential care Home encourages relatives and friends to visit at any time. a private visitor's lounge is available if needed and refreshments are provided.

BENEFITS ASSISTANCE
Specialist help is provided to deal with DSS claims for suitable applicants.

For further information please contact: Mrs. Elaine Habbershaw, Manageress

Epilogue

Hornsea's census figures suggest that there was a lull in the development of the town in the two decades before 1891. After the big rise in population that occurred with the coming of the railway to Hornsea, the increase in each of the next two decades was under 10%, a figure slightly less than the national increase. It would seem that Hornsea's population was no more than keeping pace with the rise due to the improving health of the nation. However, there were changes in the make-up of the population of the town.

In the 15 years before the 1891 census Britain had been in recession due to foreign competition. Agriculture, in particular, was seriously affected. Many men left farming and moved to the towns, and in some purely agricultural parishes, such as nearby Bewholme and Nunkeeling, the population actually went down between 1881 and 1891. In Hornsea there was probably a shift in population, with the loss of agriculturalists being made up by an increase in the numbers of Hull commuters and others coming to serve their needs and those of the holiday trade. That well-to-do people were still being attracted to Hornsea is indicated by the fact that both the census return and the 1891 Ordnance Survey map show that new houses were being built in what is now Eastbourne Road. Thus, although Hornsea's population was no more than keeping up with the natural increase, the balance was changing towards a wealthier class of inhabitant.

However, new residents were not exactly flooding into Hornsea, despite all the things that should have made the town attractive — easy communication with Hull, water and gas on tap, sewage removal, street lighting and street cleaning — all of which had been established by the end of the seventies. In a time of recession, it may be that many prospective residents were loath to pay the rates that such amenities required. The Hull commuters who did come to reside in Hornsea were probably considerably well-off.

The surge in population that accompanied the opening of railway communications, and the coming of a wealthier class of inhabitant, brought a swift improvement to the fortunes of all four religious denominations in the town. Even as the railway was being projected the Primitive Methodists had plans for a new chapel. Within a few years of the arrival of the railway, all four denominations had spent considerable sums on new buildings or renovations. New educational establishments were also attracted to the town, catering for those inhabitants who wished their children to have a better education than that provided by the old-established National School. The new schools also attracted boarders, the children of parents who no doubt saw in Hornsea a healthy place for their offspring to live whilst being educated.

Thus, although Hornsea's development had slowed, the town can be seen as establishing itself as a better-class place for Hull business and professional men to live, either in the new housing close to the railway station or in the one or two larger residences in the quieter part of the town. Meanwhile, the older part of Hornsea became more the working-class area of the town.

With the death of Joseph Wade in 1896, the 1890s can also be seen as the end of an era in Hornsea. Joseph Armytage Wade features in many of the chapters in this book and looms large in nearly every aspect of Hornsea's history in the latter part of the 19th century. It was he who brought the railway to Hornsea in 1864. It was he who tried to establish the town as a seaside resort, especially by the building of a pier. It was he who was the prime mover in the setting-up of the Local Board of Health. He had two manufacturing concerns in the town and he was head of the larger of the two gasworks companies. He was a farmer, running his 350 acres of land by the most advanced methods of the times. With his farm and business concerns he provided considerable employment in the town. No wonder that his death was lamented by many and that his funeral was the largest attended of any ever in Hornsea. It is said that as the head of his funeral procession was entering St. Nicholas church the end was just leaving Bridge railway station, near the present Marlborough Avenue.

Not all Wade's endeavours were attended with success. His Hull and Hornsea Railway was taken over by the North Eastern Railway Company within three years of its opening. His pier project took years to come to fruition and ended in disaster. And, if we see in his pier an attempt to make Hornsea a popular seaside resort, that aim was not wholly successful. However, it was his efforts that helped to make Hornsea what it became.

Wade tried to develop Hornsea by two means: by investing his own capital and that of shareholders, and by harnessing public expenditure. His private ventures included the railway and the pier. By convincing the residents of the need for a local board he ensured that Hornsea achieved advanced public services at the expense of the rate-payer, a quite uncommon achievement for a small community in the 1860s. His gasworks, intended primarily for street-lighting, were a private enterprise, but only after an attempt, probably by Wade, to have them built and controlled by the parish. As Hornsea developed, Wade benefited from the enhanced price of the land he owned in the town and the demand on his brickworks when the many new houses began to spring up.

When his last private venture to develop Hornsea — the pier — ended in 1880, Wade may have felt that further private efforts by him were no longer needed, and that he could direct Hornsea's fortunes from his position as chairman of the Local Board of Health. The board, however, and later, the Urban District Council, represented a more democratic way in which a community could be developed. In the course of time it came to contain other influential men, men who looked on Hornsea as their place of residence and perhaps a resort for the better class of visitor, but not a place to be developed at all costs. Their outlook, together with the recession, may have combined to slow down the pace of Hornsea's development. That it was only a lull in the town's progress, however, is shown by the fact that in the decades ending 1901, 1911 and 1921, Hornsea's population rose by 18%, 27% and 42% respectively. Why this happened is a story for another book, and for someone else to tell.

For the very best

Fish and Chips cooked especially for you by:

Butterworths of Hornsea

Cliffe Road, Telephone (0964) 534231

Hornsea Plumbing & Kitchen Centre

DIY and fully fitted kitchens bedrooms, bathrooms and showers

All plumbing and electrical needs, fridges, freezers, cookers (both fitted and free standing) by "Zanussi" "The appliance of science"

consult Dave Hornby

**142A Newbegin, Hornsea
Tel: (0964) 535560**

---

unicorn

**55A NEWBEGIN
HORNSEA
534527**

Proprietor: Lesley Topliss

Candles, Fashion Jewellery
Crystals, Myth and Magic
Aromatherapy, Gem Stones and
Tie Dye Indian Cotton Print Skirts
and Jackets

Always a warm welcome at

THE ICE BOX

A large selection of top brands of frozen foods and long life microwave meals always in stock

57 NEWBEGIN, HORNSEA
Telephone 532068

SOMETHING SPECIAL

For all your freshly baked bread, confectionery and savouries produced here on the premises.

**High Class Bakers and Confectioners
22 Cliff Road, Hornsea. Tel: 535979**

THE HOT SPOT
COVERED FOR COMFORT!

Wilbur's Market

EVERY SUNDAY AND WEDNESDAY

and Bank Holidays too!

COME ON DOWN AND ENJOY THE NEW SHOPPING EXPERIENCE, MAKE A DATE TO JOIN YOUR FRIENDS AT WILBUR'S - COME EARLY!

Enjoy your day at The Happy Market by the seaside

SANDS LANE, HORNSEA
Tel: 0964 532549

MIDLAND

Midland Bank plc

22 Newbegin
Hornsea

THE LISTENING BANK

For all your Motoring Requirements

Wide selection of gifts for the enthusiasts

Call and see

A and M

18 Newbegin, Hornsea
Telephone 535119

THE AUTHORS. Hornsea W.E.A. Local History Class, 1992-3. Left to right, back row: Bernard Wise, Harry Sharp, Geoff Strangward, William Browning, Maitland Smith, Alf Maltby, George White, Les Jackson; front row: Pat Browning, Maureen Mallison, Peggy Wood, Anne Malley, Joan Wise.